GREAT DAMES

WOMEN SHARING
THEIR POWER

52 True Stories Collected by
Sharon Kelly Hake with Kathy Palokoff

GREAT DAMES®
KINDRED SPIRITS WITH PURPOSE

Published by Great Dames Fund, Inc.
Philadelphia, PA
www.GreatDames.com
info@Great-Dames.com

ISBN: 9798850417802

Printed in the United States of America.

Disclaimer: This book depicts real-life scenarios of individual contributors, and some content may be triggering or distressing. If you need support, please seek help or advice from appropriate professionals. Although this publication is designed to provide accurate information, the publisher and contributors assume no responsibility for errors, inaccuracies, omissions, or any other inconsistencies.

Cover & Book Design by Jesse Baker

*This book is dedicated to the Great Dames of the world
who activate our 'Great Dameness' by inspiring us
to forge powerful connections, share stories,
and discover our voice and power.*

"The courage it takes to share your story might be the very thing someone else needs to open their heart to hope."
— *Unknown*

Table of Contents

Foreword

By Andra Rush

There are so many things about *Great Dames: Women Sharing Their Power* that resonate with me. The storytelling. The powerful women. The generosity of sharing experiences with others. The multi-generational perspectives. These are important parts of both my own Native American heritage and my core value of helping women find their power.

Storytelling is an essential part of Indigenous cultures. Stories teach us about our history and traditions. They connect the past, present, and future. They strengthen our values and truth. They form our worldview. They tighten tribal and familial bonds. Traditionally, our stories were passed from one generation to another through the spoken word. Today, many Native Americans use the written word to share contemporary experiences with the world. The Great Dames in this book come from so many different backgrounds and cultures, but they share the belief that their stories are valuable to help others grow and thrive. They want to share their power.

Strong, powerful women run in my family. My Mohawk grandmother, Minnie Alice Maracle, worked three jobs as a maid and felt deep pride in her ability to support the family with my grandfather. When I was just a young child, she told me, "You have Mohawk blood so that makes you special and rare. It will help you in all that you do. When you are running a race or putting your mind to something, you will win." She provided me with a foundation of confidence and deep pride in my heritage.

I remember one trip back to the reservation when I was 16. My grandmother pointed to a tree and told me it was my great-great-great grandmother's tree. "It's still here and has life and memory. Remember it." The tree represented strength and patience to her, and she passed those lessons on to me. She also was firm about standing up to the rampant discrimination against our people. It was instrumental in me becoming an advocate for what is right and a fighter against what is wrong.

My mother was very much my French grandmother's daughter. She fiercely guarded her independence, while planning for the worst and hoping for the best. Her influence kept me level-headed and humble. She, like my grandmother, enjoyed people for who they were and worked hard not to be judgmental. She was very encouraging of her children, which was an important reason why we were all successful in our careers.

I personally went from being a nurse to becoming the founder and CEO of one of the largest Native American, women-owned manufacturing companies in the United States. My position has enabled me to help change the trajectory of thousands of people's lives by providing training, jobs, and opportunities. My ability to do this came from finding my own power as a woman leader, despite working in an industry that was heavily male dominated. To do this, I sought out the support of remarkable women and men, as did so many of the people in this book.

In Native American heritage, nothing is yours. It's the world's. It's the universe's. Growing up, my family had a hard work ethic that has stayed with me today. But we had an equally hard giving ethic. If I had 10 cents in my pocket and you said you needed 11 cents, I'd give you my 10 and find another penny.

The authors who participated in *Great Dames: Women Sharing Their Power* have this same generosity of spirit. No one in the Great Dames community was obligated to share their story, yet they saw it as an obligation to reach out to others with their own life experiences and hope it would make the universe better. They let their stories fly free.

I also love that the authors come from so many different generations with ages from 17 to 87. There is a Native American philosophy called "The Seventh Generation." We are asked to think and act and in ways that benefit the seventh generation coming after us and honor the seventh generation who came before us. Today many environmentalists apply this principle about energy, water, and natural resources to ensure decisions are sustainable for seven generations into the future. My own passion and goals concern water conservation and use.

I believe the women who wrote this book would appreciate Seventh Generation. We are all deeply interconnected and part of this living planet – Mother Earth. Our power to do good for people and planet is all that truly matters.

Andra Rush is the founder and chairperson of The Rush Group family of companies.

Introduction

By Sharon Kelly Hake

"I can breathe again." Those words were delivered by Mia, a young woman who attended a 2015 Great Dames conversation event where we talked about the power of mentorship and having someone in your corner whom you could really count on. She was new to our group, and this was her first meeting. When the audience was invited to contribute, she stood up quickly and said those four words.

Silence followed. Mia then told us she had not planned to attend because she had a lot on her plate. But she was glad she did, because she could breathe again despite everything she was trying to deal with in her life. The women in the room had given her the oxygen she needed to thrive.

Mia was a single mother who worked full-time and attended a university part-time. She did not have any free time, but a friend convinced her she should come to a Great Dames event. She said she did not have a lot of support in her life but felt supported when she entered the room, even though she did not know the women.

We were sisters in spirit that evening.

I will never forget her words, nor the woman who said them. Hearing Mia confirmed what I deeply believed about women: When women come together, great things happen. And when women share their stories with one another, even greater things happen. Women thrive when we are surrounded by women we can trust. Women who value us for our wisdom and experiences. Women who help us discover our value, our voice, our power. Each of us gains and shares power when we convene and connect deeply through our stories, wisdom, and experiences.

Great Dames was founded to convene women so they could forge meaningful connections and deep friendships. To help them be trusted sounding boards for the ideas, fears, and challenges of other women. To form a community that would respond to each other with openness and without judgment.

It was an idea that I contemplated for a long time. I craved a world where women found support, friendship, and positive reinforcement from other women. Where women were mentored, motivated, and held accountable. Where we were valued for our ideas, and our desire to create a unique impact on the world. Where we believed in our individual and collective power to create change. Over time, I began to imagine how extraordinary it would be to create this kind of community.

Working with my daughters, Heather and Deirdre, and thousands of Dames, we created a global community of women who are committed to ensuring that all women have the opportunity to discover their 'Great Dameness.' During the last 15 years, we have come together to connect, support, learn, and lead through conversation. We've shared our challenges and accomplishments, but mostly we've listened, nurtured, empathized, and believed.

We created this book to provoke us to think differently, enlighten us to be more empathetic, challenge us to act, and encourage us to love ourselves completely. As a community, we wanted to share our powerful stories and experiences to benefit others. We are honored that more than fifty women from our global community participated.

In this book, we explore the power of women's storytelling and how it helps us connect with each other, challenge our thinking, and effect change. We hear from women from all walks of life, from diverse cultures and backgrounds. We discover how these women have used their stories to inspire others, promote social justice, and empower themselves and their communities. This book is a celebration of women's resilience, strength, and creativity, and a call to action for all women to share their stories and make their voices heard.

We are women kindred spirits. We are Great Dames.

Sharon Kelly Hake is founder of Great Dames, a global community of women who are committed to discovery, empowerment, friendship, and creating impact by forging deep connections with other women.

What's in a Name?

By Lele Galer

What's in a name? In my case, my ridiculously spelled nickname is a combination of tragedy, ignorance, guile, and just bad luck. Bad luck is being the third girl when no one would have thought that the third attempt for a III would be yet another girl. In my family, for many generations, the male has kept the same name and once it gets to III, it reverts back to the start again. III shows lineage, but IV, V, and so on is just vulgar.

My father was a Jr., so the next male child would be a III.

My paternal grandmother pleaded for my mother to name the next child after her, Louise, as she had pleaded for every girl baby thus far. With this final plea, however, she added the extra little treat that the namesake would inherit more, whatever that meant. My mother promised to do so this time around — my time around — never thinking that she would be so unlucky as to have a third girl. Yet here I was, and although she would have had no guilt about skirting her promise to her mother-in-law, my mother was actually at a loss for names that interested her, and the extra possibility of inheritance was too enticing to ignore.

But, as she looked over at her beautiful baby girl through the veil of her groggy, drug-induced stupor, she thought "Hell, no. I just delivered this child, and that bitch isn't going to get her way." But she had promised, and more importantly, money was involved. The attending nurse had just brought me into her private room, which full of vases of flowers, and I was settled, wrapped tightly, in a rectangular cabinet next to my mother. My mother looked at me but had no desire to hold me. She had wanted a boy and got another girl, but I looked healthy and would be pretty enough. Well, who could tell really, but she was beautiful, and her husband was handsome, so chances were very good that I would be pretty, at least.

But she certainly was not naming this child Louise. A quiet grin took over and she would have laughed out loud if she hadn't been afraid of anyone overhearing her. She'd name the baby Louise all right, but she'd put that in the middle. She'd put her own mother's name in front, so it would be Anna Louise, and when the baby wed, the Louise part would be dropped from existence. My mom herself was married at 20 (too young, she thought now). Say this baby Louise was married at 22; 22 years from now, surely Mom's mother-in-law would be dead. One could only hope.

In any case, mother-in-law would owe the inheritance, but she should have been more specific about what inheritance. It had been stupid of Mom not to ask for details, but she didn't know how to press the question without sounding needy or lower-class. The troublesome thought was quickly pushed from her thoughts. If she'd known how to ask more specifically, then she would have, but her dear, entitled husband never talked about those sorts of things.

Never talk about money. Never ask. Live like it never came up and never mattered — but it mattered all the time. It was up to her to secure their rights, what her children were due.

So, I would be named Anna Louise, even though my mother hated her mother Anna, who was not a part of her life; in fact, she decided then and there that she wasn't going to tell her mother that she had named a child for her. This was about spite, not about honor. Her mother was part of a distasteful memory of her entire existence before marriage. She hadn't spoken to her in years. How could someone like her have been

2

born of such inconsequential people? It made her feel sick to even think of calling this child Anna.

No, they could skirt the whole dilemma by calling me some sort of nickname. My father must have entered the room at some point, coming in to congratulate my mother on the birth of another girl. Lord knows where he had spent the night. Dads in those days didn't participate in the birthing process.

Actually, my mother was knocked out and I was delivered by forceps. I always wondered if I was worth that bit of butchery, but then I figured that my two horrible sisters had come before me and done the same, and I know for sure that they weren't worth it because they are truly awful people. So, I guess, damage done.

My father took a seat by the bed and made approving comments about the loveliness that was me and the radiance of my mother. He asked about the name, saying that he guessed it was Louise. Then, with a smile, "Yes," said my mother, pausing and then smiling with teeth: "Anna Louise, after both our mothers." She gave a loving look at me, the baby in the box. My father felt uncomfortable enough at the idea of birth and all the pain that his wife had just gone through while he'd just had a couple drinks with his friends at the club. He was out of his depth.

He didn't care what the baby was named, but hadn't she promised his mother? He certainly didn't want another disagreeable conversation between the two of them. He also didn't want to bring it up.

"I was thinking we could give her a nickname. Your mother was always called by a nickname," offered my mother. "Oh, you want to call her Lulu?" asked Dad with some surprise, guessing, hoping, that maybe they would all get along fine after all. His mother would like a baby Lulu. He smiled and then furrowed his brow. Did he get that right or wrong? He never knew what his wife was getting at, and he didn't care, and she'd just had a baby, for God's sake.

"Oh no, not Lulu," my grandmother reacted disdainfully. She

grimaced, then smiled, explaining that that name was taken. Was the grimace of disgust for the nickname or for my mother, he wondered. He just couldn't be bothered figuring out her nuances and he couldn't be anything but reassuring and sympathetic. Really a shame it wasn't a boy, although he shouldn't think like that. Poor woman, just look at her and all she has gone through, he thought.

"Lili, Lilly.... Hang on a minute, don't you mean to call her Louise Anna?" my father asked suddenly. "No," she said firmly.

"So, when she is married, she'd be Anna, not Louise ...?"

"Yes," replied my mother, patting down her blankets, slightly twitching with pain, but persevering.

There was my mother, propped up in bed, surrounded by flowers, next to a box with a baby in it that she hadn't looked at since he had walked into the room. *She is playing at some sort of power game with my mother,* he thought, *and it never stops! And she's doing that smile at me like she is beguiling me, but she doesn't know that it doesn't work anymore, and she simply scares the crap out of me. What the hell is she playing at? This is no way for me to feel right now. She just gave birth to my child! She can name her whatever she wants.*

"Whatever you want," Dad said. "Maybe there is a friend of yours called Lily?" He wanted to be the supportive husband, but he never knew how to act around her. Whatever he did was wrong, but he was full of love right now; a new baby, lovely, and this was his wife and his life, and this was right. He smiled and got on the bed and reached out for her hand. She kept her hand there for as long as she could stand it, but couldn't he see that she was repulsed?

She was beautiful, she knew that, and every man wanted to touch her. A gift and a curse, she said to herself so often, round and roundabout in her head. This is the man she had decided to devote her life to, a man who wasn't even sure he should hold her hand, couldn't even guess that she had just won a game of wits with his mother. She was better than his mother. She was better than him. She was better than this world that she'd settled for and as the drugs started to wear off a bit, she was just ticked off.

He sat by her now, looking at the baby, so perfect and beautiful, and his heart opened wide that she was his. She was so perfectly sweet. My mother looked at the dopey expression on his face as he looked away from her and stared wide-eyed at the baby that she had made. It was all her. She had done all this for him, this dopey-looking fool of a man with his controlling, overbearing mother and everything handed to him since he was born.

Even with all that, they were still struggling to make ends meet. Big house but not enough servants, clubs but not enough cash, and clothing that was handed down from his twice-married (slut), wealthy and entitled mother. She should have married Harold. He didn't have the old social register pedigree, but he had adored her, and life would have been different, better. My father looked over at my mother, with that distant, undiscoverable expression on her face. *I do not know this woman*, he thought. *I should have married Lili if she had lived.*

"How about Lili?" he said, with as innocent an expression as he could muster.

"Lili. That is pretty. Your mother won't mind?" my mother asked with as innocent expression as she could muster.

And they both smiled at each other. Thinking each had won their subterfuge, and thus I was born and named into this world. In a mixture of spite, a hunger for power, in an ocean of sadness, I was named.

To cap it off, when I was 3, I asked my older sister how to spell my name and she recited "L-e-l-e," and it stuck. A misspelling of a name. My mother didn't care and thought the cuteness of this misspelling was testament to the warm and easy-going nature of her happy household. It would be a sweet story she could recite. My father didn't care, but was relieved, because it helped to hide deeper his forever sadness at losing the love of his youth to a car crash that he didn't like to think about, but

5

somehow came to his lips when he looked at me — his third girl, who was supposed to be a boy, his III.

Lele Galer is a painter, sculptor and writer who lives in West Chester, Pennsylvania where she also runs the family winery Galer Estate Vineyard and Winery and is involved with projects and programs that promote the arts and education.

You're Just Not the Right Fit

By Gemma Lowery

"Hi, there," my supervisor says. "Can you meet me in the conference room? I want to catch up with you since I am just getting back from vacation."

"Sure," I say. "Be right there."

I walk in and notice that an HR rep is in the room with her. Instantly, I am on the defensive and wonder what the heck is going on. My supervisor starts asking me questions about my work. Nothing of any consequence in my mind; just general stuff. Then she says, "Let me get to the point of the meeting. After three years, we just don't think you are the right fit for the team."

"Excuse me? You what?"

"We wanted to bring you in to let you know we are letting you go, effective immediately."

"But I just won an award and received a bonus check two weeks ago. What changed? How can you do this to me?" I am completely confused. "Is there anything I can do to change this decision?"

"No. The rest of the team has been pulled away from the unit so you can pack up your desk in private. Then I will walk you to your car."

Does she expect me to thank her as if she is doing me a favor? No wonder my colleagues call her the grim reaper behind her back. The HR rep, who had made my life a living hell since she found out I was pregnant when they hired me, watches with a smirk on her face.

The tears start to fall, which makes me furious. No way do I want to show any weakness or let them know how devastated I am. I pull myself together and ask if they want a summary of what I am working on, since I do not want my clients to be affected by such a sudden change. They don't deserve that. I build relationships, not just clients. My now former supervisor is shocked that I would consider my clients. "No, I am sure we can figure it out," she says.

I quickly pack my things and walk to the car with her by my side. Her last comment is to commend me on my professionalism and wish me well. Had she expected me to flip out and carry on so she could call security? She still knows nothing about me after three years.

I sit there in my car in shock for a few minutes. I don't know who might be watching, so I start the car and drive home on autopilot. Nothing like this has ever happened to me. No warning. No nothing.

When I get to my house, I call my husband to tell him what happened.

"Didn't you just win an award and receive a bonus?"

"Yup."

"How can they do this to you?"

"It is an 'at will' state. They don't have to give a reason."

"What are we going to do now?"

"I don't know, but I am never working for corporate America again. Never."

"That sounds good, but what are we supposed to do now? You have to replace your salary ASAP."

The list of all the things at risk starts to flow from him to me. It's just too much. It's only been an hour. "Stop, just stop. I need time to figure this out. You aren't helping. We lose our medical coverage in three weeks, and I have to cancel my surgery. I need to think. Please, leave me alone to think."

I hang up and completely break down. Who am I without a job? I always carry my own weight. I've been working at least one job since I was 14 years old. This can't be happening to me.

The next few days go by in a haze. I am not this incapacitated person. I am the planner between us, but there is no plan for this. I am a fixer. How do I fix this?

I file for unemployment, which gives me a little bit of time to figure something out. My husband can't make any more than what he currently makes, so that option is off the table. He picks up everyone on his insurance — thank God, because our three kids have health challenges. The youngest isn't even 3 yet. What if I stay home with him until he starts kindergarten? I have friends who are starting their families. What if I watch their babies?

I start researching what it would take and know there is no time to become certified. This has to be fast and informal babysitting. It takes some convincing, but my husband agrees. He knows this is going to change how our household runs, but it is a good solution for now and will replace a portion of my income.

Two friends agree to have me watch their kiddos. I just have to hang on until their babies arrive. We have a plan. Unemployment should get us through until then.

Then I get the notice in the mail. My unemployment has been denied because I was "terminated due to poor work performance." Not a chance in hell. Now I am furious! They are not going to get away with this. How do I file an appeal? We can't afford an attorney.

Knowledge is power, and I learn from every source I can find about how to fight this decision. And surprise, surprise, my former employer has a history of this behavior.

I gather every file, note, and memory about my three years of work and the horribly hostile and vengeful environment I lived and even managed to thrive in. I realize that what started out as an exciting new career opportunity became somewhere to work and watch my back. It was never somewhere that I felt overly comfortable, but that never stopped me from doing good work. I busted my butt in a space that had so few who looked like me. I made sure I always did more than my share even when it went unrecognized.

Four months later, I finally have my mediation date. The mediator and I are in a room, waiting for their HR rep to show up. We wait and wait with no call or message until she finally arrives, 45 minutes late. The mediator is not pleased. He begins to ask questions when she stops him and asks if she can present her information first. He agrees since time is tight. After she presents, he looks at her and asks if that is it. He is angry and says she has wasted their time. He is going to write a report about how the system was used as a weapon against me to deny my claim.

I am shocked. I didn't have to present a single piece of evidence. He says that their reputation for pulling stuff like this is well-known, and he will not be a party to it. He orders immediate payment of my back pay and the remaining weeks of my entitled payments to continue without interruption. I am worthy of this compensation, and he was going to make them do the right thing by me. The power dynamic had shifted.

The HR rep looks shocked and embarrassed at the dressing down she receives in front of me. I think it is completely fair after what they did. Karma in real time is quite something to see.

I am so glad I ignored advice to "just move on and take my losses" because "you can't win against big business." Winning vindicated and validated me in a way that walking away never would have done. I would have wondered "what if?"

I have always been a fighter to a certain degree. But now I knew that I could rise when flattened to my lowest point. I had been tested in fire and became stronger, if more jaded, than before.

I did find ways to making babysitting work. I was also the crazy couponing lady and the mom who maximized every free outing and service I could find. The kids never knew how close we came to not making it. We did whatever we needed to do to make sure they had fun and were fed, clothed, safe, and loved.

I ended up getting a part-time job in health care because one of the moms I babysat for was a recruiter and desperately needed to fill a position. When the kids I watched grew older and did not need my services, I took a full-time job as a unit clerk in the hospital's ICU to determine whether I wanted to go back and get a nursing degree at age 40. I quickly concluded that I did not. Instead, I focused on my interest in technology and telehealth, and developed that knowledge and skills.

When the pandemic hit, my career skyrocketed because of the demand for virtual solutions. I am now the technology manager of digital solutions and have been with my company for 17 years. Yes, I am back in corporate America—but I am much savvier.

The life lesson badge I earned isn't one that anyone else can see, but it means more to me than just about anything I own. My determination, perseverance, knowledge of self-worth, and desire to help others from being railroaded or abused remains and continues to grow to this day.

And I absolutely know that I am exactly the right fit!

Gemma Lowery holds a master's in healthcare administration and is a healthcare access advocate focusing on telehealth. She believes that without equal, equitable and just healthcare for all, everyone suffers.

Shining the Light on Bias

By Dr. Angela Marshall

As an African American woman primary care doctor who has seen more than fifty thousand patients in the last 20 years, I have a different perspective on healthcare than many other people. And you can also add my own life lessons from experiences with prejudice, racism, and classism.

While I have taken visible leadership roles in women's health, when COVID began its course of devastation and Black Lives Matter entered mainstream America, I realized that I needed to raise my voice even louder to offer perspectives and solutions on the disparities in our healthcare system.

I decided to write a book aimed at both doctors and patients, called *Dismissed: Tackling the Biases that Undermine Our Health Care*. I chose the title *Dismissed* because it captured the emotion of so many vulnerable people when facing the healthcare system. It certainly captured how I felt. For the first time, I talked publicly about a life event that shaped my life as a doctor. I have to tell you: It took a lot of courage for me to do this. Sharing the stories of others and the research that showed the cost and potential solutions of bias was one thing. Telling my own story made me feel very vulnerable, but I knew it was necessary for people to really listen to the message I was delivering.

My second son was born with posterior urethral valves, a condition that caused my newborn's kidneys and lungs to develop poorly, resulting in the need for immediate heart and lung support after birth and dialysis a few days later — a condition we found out about when I was five months pregnant. After two months in the hospital, Nathan was stable enough to be discharged to home so he could qualify for a kidney transplant when he was six months old. A world-renowned pediatric kidney specialist at our local children's hospital monitored his progress.

I had just finished my fourth year of medical school with only a one-month rotation left to graduate. Nathan's birth was planned so I would have nine months off to care for my baby. It was a labor of love to help rehabilitate him back to good health, and he was progressing nicely. He was receiving home dialysis, and physical and occupational therapy. Then one day, when I was getting Nathan ready for his scheduled appointment with the specialist, I noticed he didn't seem like himself. He was unresponsive, staring into space with his eyes crossing in different directions.

I rushed him to the hospital, calling ahead to inform them that something seemed really wrong and thankful that he already had an appointment that morning. His doctor said Nathan would have to be admitted to the hospital to start treatment, but there were no beds available. He didn't seem to feel the urgency that I did, but he hadn't seen the eye-crossing thing I had witnessed, although I explained it in great detail. In fact, the doctor looked doubtful.

When Nathan's vitals were checked, I realized he was even sicker than I thought. His respiratory rate was 100 times per minute, while a normal respiratory rate is between 30 and 60. I had learned from my pediatrics rotation that the breathing rate in children is an important indicator of illness and one of the most important vital signs of infants.

There was no room available at that moment. After waiting for more than half an hour, I began to ask about the status of the room. When were they going to actually start treating my son? I was told they were still waiting for the room, and I explained that I didn't think we had much time to wait. "How long can he keep breathing at 100 times per minute?" I asked. Finally, I raised my voice: "He needs help *now!*"

One nurse seemed to understand my urgency. She even expressed her own concerns. She called the doctor, but he kept dismissing both of us. He finally came back into the room and, without examining Nathan, said, "Look, I've been doing this for 30 years. His electrolytes are out of balance because he is sick. But as soon as we get him to a room and give him fluids, we'll get him tanked up, and he'll be back to his normal self in no time."

Something about the doctor reminding me of his 30 years of experience made me breathe a sigh of relief. In fact, I even felt a bit embarrassed that I had been raising my voice. I wanted to advocate for my son, but I did not want to appear ungrateful, nor did I want to overreact. After all, I was a medical student, and he was an experienced doctor who had cared for many very sick children. The doctor had it under control. He was a world-renowned kidney specialist with decades of experience. I even told my husband he could go home and gather our things because it was just a waiting game.

Then the nurse returned to check Nathan one more time. During the exam, my baby stopped breathing. She called a Code Blue. Nathan's heart had stopped. She told me we had to do CPR. I immediately started breathing into his mouth while crying hysterically. It seemed a lifetime between our starting CPR and the arrival of the code team. I was ushered out of the room and into the hallway, where I prayed harder than I ever have in my life.

Nathan did not make it. My life was shattered. I cannot even find the words to describe how difficult it was to go back to the same hospital to complete my rotation one month after he died, but I had no choice. I knew that no matter how painful, I had to graduate medical school because I had a very clear mission: to practice medicine in a different way so no one would ever go through what I had.

I don't know why Nathan's doctor dismissed me and would not listen to my repeated concerns. Was it because I was a woman? Was it the color of my skin? Did he not want to be challenged by a med student? Was he burnt out? Was he arrogant because of his past accomplishments? Was he simply having a bad day? I don't know the answer. But every day I feel the loss that resulted from his dismissal of the person who knew Nathan best: his mother.

Since taking this intensely personal story public, I have experienced such a connection with others who have been dismissed in healthcare, the workplace, and society in general. My story resonated with them in a big way. Sometimes, their dismissal was about race. Other times, it was due to gender, age, weight, or disabilities. Often, more than one bias factor figured into how they were treated. My hope for reducing dismissal was articulated in my book dedication: "This book is dedicated to my children, husband, patients, and the next generation. May they live in a world where they are never dismissed."

My message is spreading through book sales, media interviews, speaking engagements, and more. Let me be honest. Writing my book and telling my story was a very intense and time-consuming experience. But it was necessary and fulfilling. While I am focused on institutional and societal change, if one doctor or one patient's life is made better by my bringing this issue to light, I will have accomplished something important.

I urge you to raise your own voice to be heard. Whatever injustice you see and are experiencing, do not remain silent. That is where your power lies.

Dr. Angela Marshall is the founder of Comprehensive Women's Health, a primary care practice for women, and Comprehensive Aesthetics and Bodywork. A changemaker in healthcare, she is the author of Dismissed: Tackling the Biases that Undermine Our Healthcare.

Everything and Anything

By Bradley Beck

Manure never smelled like shit when I shoveled it with my Gramp. It was sweet and musty, pleasantly pungent, and dried-flower floral. Hauling manure every spring at my grandparents' farm was one of my favorite times. One of many.

Gramp grew up through the Depression and World War II rationing. His stories were of hunting and fishing, not for sport but to feed the family; of digging holes and then filling them back in for work with the Conservation Corps; of planting and tending massive gardens, not as a hobby but for food to make it through the winter.

He was a farmer, carpenter, plumber, electrician, mechanic, welder, veterinarian, butcher, entrepreneur, hunter, trapper, fisherman, cook.

In my young eyes, he knew about everything, could fix anything, do anything.

"Aim for right between the eyes." My only fear was missing and disappointing Gramp. Ricky was the young steer Gramp had given me to take care of, to fatten up for slaughter. It was time. Life and death on the farm was the natural cycle.

"Go get us a chicken for dinner," Grandma would say, handing me a small club. "Just hit its head." Pulling the chicken from scalding hot water and plucking its feathers, she pointed out the bruises where I missed.

The miracle. It never seemed to fail. Till, plant, fertilize, cultivate, pray for rain, harvest. Winter wheat and oats in July. Hay all summer. Corn, soybeans, vegetables in October. Perpetually dirty greasy hands; churning harvest machines; sweaty, weary bodies; battles with mud and mechanics.

The bounty safely in the barn and in our hearts.

The intertwining of earth and animals, of gratitude and respect, of love. Palpable at every meal. Inescapable when eating a Ricky roast, when the bacon and eggs came from the hen house and hog coup, when the rabbit stew or frog legs came from hunting with my Gramp, when the vegetables came from the land I stood on.

Pure unfettered youthful discovery and joy. Unknowingly, my seed of deep connection to the earth, nature, life, death, family. It sprouted and grew.

I believed I could know about everything, fix anything, do anything.

Brad Beck, a Great Dames male ally, believes: Writing is an intimate way for me to reflect, explore and think. Reflection always makes me grateful for the amazing women in my life. The world would be better if more women were in charge.

Words from My Father

By Sharon Kelly Hake

My father never wasted a word in his life. His words were, and still are, often quoted by family, friends, colleagues, and anyone else who came into his life. Through his words, he taught me many things, including how to be a friend, develop deep empathy, listen, learn, and create an impact.

Even though my father was fairly small in stature, his presence was felt whenever he entered the room. People would stop talking and turn in his direction, knowing he'd share a memorable story, a witty remark, or words of wisdom. He had so many insights, earned from a lifetime of challenges and accomplishments.

When I'm in a difficult place, I often say these four words: "What would Dad say?" And I can usually find an answer from among the words he shared with me. I miss his presence tremendously, but I can still hear his powerful words.

"Children, what did you do today to justify your existence?"

I grew up in a large Irish Catholic family of nine: seven kids with two parents who probably wondered what the heck they had created together. Dinner was a command performance, and our presence was expected. Our conversations were so stimulating that we gladly made it home, especially for the lively dinner discussions over several pots of tea, as we debated, argued, entertained, and laughed together.

My father would usually ask each of his children the same question when the conversation got quiet during dinner: "Children, what did you do today to justify your existence?" Those 10 words packed a wallop. We knew by his demeanor that it was an important question, but it was a tough one to answer, especially at a young age. As he repeatedly asked each of us the same question, we began to understand that he was teaching us a powerful lesson: We are each here for a purpose, and we needed to figure out what that purpose was. No free rides. We needed to continuously look for opportunities to make a positive impact on the world. He was counting on us to do that. Always.

"You're right, life isn't fair. And you've had an unfair advantage!"

Our dinnertime conversations often included complaints from several of us who believed that something unfair had happened to them that day. Someone was being picked on, mistreated, asked to do something extra, or cheated out of some recognition or prize. The offended person would usually declare, "That isn't fair!"

My father had a strong response to that declaration. "You're right, life isn't fair. And you've had an unfair advantage!" Eleven words. He'd go on to say that our unfair advantage included being born into our family and community with food on the table, a roof over our heads, and parents who loved us. This was entirely unfair because many people did not have all those things, and we did. That pretty much shut us up.

"Don't tell me about your accomplishments.
Tell me what your friends say about you."

My father often admonished us with this when we were busy bragging about ourselves. His powerful words are seared in my brain. If I don't know what my friend says or feels, how can I be a true friend to them? And my father had many friends, because he had a tremendous capacity for relationships based on commitment and trust.

He often talked about the importance of friendship and believed that you could never have too many friends. He observed that no one would by angry with you if you befriended them. Nice solves everything. Interestingly, he had more friends — good friends — than anyone I knew. And he stayed connected to them all at a very deep level. He was a generous friend, and he treated every one of his friends as a gift.

"What's love got to do with it?"

My father was an upbeat person. He always assumed positive intent, so he was generally able to create common ground with people in his life. One day, he came home with a very disturbed look on his face. When we asked him about it, he said his close friend, George, was leaving Alice, his wife of more than 25 years. My father was shocked and saddened to hear the news and asked him why. When George replied that he just didn't love Alice anymore, my father responded, "What's love got to do with it?" Seven words. George was absolutely stumped.

We have shared this story many times, and it usually generate gales of laughter. At least initially. Yet when I think more deeply about it, I realize that in those seven words, my father was teaching us that commitment meant commitment. People change and circumstances change, but our commitment to each other is the overriding force. We need to decide to love, even when it's difficult thing to do. I often reflect on those seven words when I hit a dry patch with an important person in my life, and I look for ways to reinvigorate our relationship. I'm usually successful. It's all about deciding to love.

"Travel is the best form of education."

My father loved to travel, and he visited many places around the world for business and pleasure. He also planned a family vacation every summer with the whole gang, even when money was tight and time off was scarce. We looked forward to those outings because we knew we'd meet new people, hear unusual accents, see amazing sights, and experience different cultures.

During those road trips, I'd often hear my father say, "Travel is the best form of education." When I reflect on those seven words, I realize that he was talking about empathy. Travel takes us out of our comfort zone and forces us to be in someone else's shoes — to see the world from their eyes and to learn something worth learning.

"The only person you can't hide from is yourself."

My father was a fearless debater who won most arguments in our household with his smart comebacks in the face of seven kids who were trying to prove their point. He was also brutally honest when he thought we were off track or blaming someone else for our mistakes. I remember telling him tales of woe about people who weren't fair or nice, or disagreed with me. He would listen intently and said, "The only person you can't hide from is yourself." Nine words.

After receiving zero sympathy from him, I would reflect on those nine words, and eventually realized that he detected a pattern to my stories: It was always the other guy's fault when I told the story, but I came to realize it was my fault for responding the way I did. My response to the situation was my responsibility. I had to look in the mirror. I could not hide from myself. That one was tough.

"Thought of you. You can do this."

When my dad died at age 76, he left behind a huge community of admirers. Hundreds attended his funeral, and his children greeted every person who came to talk about him. I noticed a distinct theme in their words of sympathy. They were going to miss their mentor, advisor, and trusted ally. Many claimed he was their best friend. He was the one they counted on to help them think through life's challenges and emerge in a better place.

I realized that my experiences and those of my siblings were shared by many others: He gave each of us what we needed when we needed it. His kids would often joke that each one of us was Dad's favorite. That's because he treated each of us as his favorite.

I remember getting a note in the mail from him at an incredibly stressful time in my life. I was a young mother in a very demanding job. His note included a *New Yorker* magazine cartoon depicting a woman in a business suit, carrying a baby and a briefcase, while racing to grab a taxi to get to a business meeting. He wrote a note that said. "Thought of you. You can do this." Seven words. I still have that note, nearly 40 years later.

Sharon Kelly Hake is founder of Great Dames, a global community of women who are committed to discovery, empowerment, friendship, and creating impact by forging deep connections with other women

The Other Side of Fear

By Sarah Kenney-Cruz

I knew, as I looked down at my notebook, that I was ready to make the biggest decision of my life. I was ready to move away from my home in Wilmington, Delaware, and take a job 600 miles away, in Indianapolis, Indiana.

I was ready to take the big interview, and ready to say "yes" if the position excited me as much in person as it did on paper. I had considered the big factors. I was married, so this decision involved my husband, who was also firmly rooted in Delaware. I was pregnant. (I didn't know *how* pregnant ...). And there were rumblings about something called COVID-19, so that was a bit of an unknown.

But as I looked down at the page where I had made my list, everything on the "pro" side was opportunity. Everything on the "con" side was fear.

I didn't make decisions based on fear anymore. I hadn't in a few years, ever since I had reported to a boss who was afraid of *everything*. It was utterly exasperating. We couldn't get anything done, because she was so busy predicting which monsters would pop out of the closet. Now, it's part of my psyche: If fear stands as the *only* thing in my way, the decision is made. I'm doing it. So, as I sat there, looking at my list, I knew I had to move forward with the interview.

My husband had been on board within a few hours — without cajoling or convincing. I had simply presented the job description and then let him think about it. He was ready for the adventure before I even fully absorbed what I was asking of him.

I brushed my fears aside and took the interview.

I crushed it. I was fueled by some fiery boss-woman, mama-to-be girl power. I wore my tightest blazer because I wasn't showing yet. I was aiming for a vibe akin to "look how *not* pregnant I am!" (always a concern when you're in your early 30s with a recent wedding photo on social media).

Everything about the job excited me: It was global, it was a different sector, and it was a new start.

They offered me the job. I negotiated. They accepted. And I knew I had to take it.

There was the hard work of telling my parents. My mother was especially upset. This would be the furthest apart we had ever been. And I was 34. There was the hard work of telling my friends. They were all lovely about it, but as an introvert, the conversations were still exhausting. And then there was the hard work of preparing to move. We had to put our Delaware residence on the market and go house-hunting in Indiana. Those trips were rushed weekend episodes, in miserable winter weather.

Then, there was the miraculous doctor's appointment where we discovered we were having not one baby, but two! Twins! I was shocked. I shouldn't have been. After all, my husband and I are both fraternal twins ourselves. But somehow, I hadn't mentally prepared for the possibility of multiples.

In addition, that little virus called COVID-19 shut down the entire world, right when we closed on our new house and moved across country — in a van loaded with boxes, a dog, and two cats. We never met the sellers. Paperwork was signed in separate rooms, with wiped-down pens and face masks. We never got to have our *moving away party* because restaurants had closed their doors and gatherings were prohibited.

I'm not going to lie — it was hard. It was *really* hard. After our beautiful, perfect babies were born, we became first-time parents in a new area, during a pandemic, with help in short supply. Three months after the babies were born, I returned to work, and navigated the landmines that all working mothers navigate: the guilt, the stress, and the concern ping-ponging through my brain at all hours. But I loved the job. The opportunity was made for me. Professionally, I was thriving.

Now, we're learning to love Indianapolis. At first, it was difficult because the pandemic limited how much we could do. Now, it's difficult because I disagree with Indiana politics. But I'm absorbing this place like a sponge and figuring out where I fit and where I can add value.

My mom is OK. I know she wishes I was in Delaware, but we enjoy visiting one another. We talk on the phone. We do FaceTime. Our relationship has evolved. And that was important to me.

God bless my husband, Dave. I can't imagine going on this adventure with anyone else. He's my partner in every single way, and he believes in me like no one else ever has.

Through this experience, I've learned that everything worthwhile really *is* on the other side of fear. I think most people already know what risk they should take — they are just trying to convince themselves otherwise. Instead of questioning yourself, take the leap. It takes the same amount of energy, but it gives you momentum into your very best future.

Sarah Kenney-Cruz is a global communications professional. She lives in Indianapolis, IN with her husband, their twins and a small menagerie of pets.

Goodness Prevails

By Johnette Hartnett, Ed.D.

When I was 33 years old, I lost my three young children and their babysitter in an early-morning house fire. The memory remains real and oddly dreamlike. Now, in my 70s, I realized that while I survived, recovery remains elusive. Although I learned to manage my life and find new meaning, I would never say I recovered.

My loss became a lifelong companion. It defined who I became. I skipped many of the traditional life cycle events enjoyed by my married friends and their families. No remarriage, no grandchildren. A new career at age 50. And the question I am repeatedly asked, even 40 years later, is "How did you survive?"

Unimaginable Loss

A bulletin interrupted the regular scheduled program on the radio. An early morning-house fire had taken the lives of three children and another, yet-unidentified person. Then I heard the location announced. We were the only family with three children who lived on that street. My body began to shake. The car sputtered because my foot was no longer steady enough to engage the clutch. And it was my house with fire trucks on the lawn and people standing on the sidewalk.

My father was there as I got out of the car. I asked him what had happened and started climbing the steps to the front porch. Firemen said I could not go in. I disagreed, and my father was by my side as we stood in the front living room of my 1850s home. Looking up, I saw exposed beams charred and dripping. It was like the house was weeping.

On the bookshelf was a row of family picture albums, now history. On the floor sat a large, empty popcorn bowl next to a game, now abandoned. The popcorn was my final gesture as a mom before I left the the night before.

I insisted on climbing the now-wobbly winding staircase, unhinged from its secure anchor to their bedrooms. The thermostats were dripping down the wall. My children and their babysitter were not there. My family was gone. My life as I knew it had ended.

I found myself next door, on my mother's couch, with a young priest from my parish by my side. He took my hand and told me God needed my three children as angels in heaven. I told him, with all due respect, that the loving God in my life did not take the lives of innocent children.

The rest is a blur. I remember walking up the steps to the church for the babysitter's funeral and being told by a kind old priest that it was not necessary for me to attend. I went in anyway, again with my father by my side.

I remember standing at the graves of my children, and someone telling me it was time to go. I do not remember how I ever walked away from my children that morning. But I did.

There were so many endings. I was no longer a mother or wife. It seemed as though my roots in small-town New England died along with my life. My religious practice of Catholicism was sadly lacking in answers that made sense. Why my children? I was no Job. My traditions and culture of couples, children, and church suppers did not know what to do for me. I was an enigma.

I became a member of a new club. I learned quickly that my story ignited one of our worst human fears: the loss of a child. For me, it was the loss of all three of my children — my two sons and daughter. I did not know how to grieve or cope. I struggled with not being home the night of the fire. Although legally separated from my husband at the time of the fire, I felt like a modern-day Scarlett O'Hara: I was consumed with guilt. I believed I was unforgivable. I should have been home. *I* should have died, not my children or their babysitter. It was indeed the dark night of my soul.

Trying to Find Meaning

Two years after the fire, I found myself in an old Buddhist monastery in the Catskills of New York with 70 other individuals, all searching for a way to understand their lives after loss. I met a young man who was gay and the father of six. He was dying. I told him we were like two actors passing in the night. He was searching for a meaningful ending. I was searching for a meaningful beginning. None of it made sense. I said if I could, I would have traded lives with him.

I listened to terminally ill people express their concerns about who would care for their aging parents or young children. One woman was obsessed with how many casseroles she could freeze before she died. I watched a young wounded warrior weep as he was welcomed home from Vietnam and thanked for his service for the first time in years. I listened to stories of depression, mental illness, cancer, disease, murder, war, accidents, death, and addiction. Even the loss of a pet. And I heard people like me, reeling from the shock of a sudden death of their beloved son or daughter.

As I closed my eyes and listened to their stories, I heard the anger, fear, shame, and regret. They were mine, too — different losses, but the same emotional responses. All with the raw and familiar broken-hearted theme. The suffering was palpable.

We learned that the process of healing was like alchemy. Our lives would be transformed, never to be the same as before our trauma. Some of us rolled our eyes at this heresy. To me, there was no hope of rising above my grief. Others felt the same about their losses. I was still steeped in the question "Why them, why not me?" Forgiveness of myself was not an option.

It came down to one common characteristic: our shared loss experiences. No matter our religion, gender, profession, or story, the focus was on our responses to loss. I began to realize that it was not my story that mattered but my response. How could I start over? How would I live without my children? Would I ever trust life again? Four decades later, I realize that most of my healing was not about the fire but about my response.

On the last night of our week together, we were asked to throw a pinecone into the fire with a message. I do not remember my message. But I do remember feeling a tiny sliver of hope for a fleeting moment. Today, I know that sliver of hope was a nudge from my new life waiting in the wings. Ironically, the week-long headline of death and dying was life-affirming.

Moving Forward

Memories of that week in the Catskills and the forgiveness I experienced began to manifest in small ways. Some mornings, I would wake up and for a few seconds, totally forget my story. I would feel hope. Then I would remember, and suddenly it would come rushing back like a dagger.

I learned to mimic these wakeful moments of *forgetfulness* and store my obsessive thoughts deep in my heart for a few minutes every hour. Month after month. Year after year. Eventually, the exercise became habit as I found a safe place for my story.

My thoughts and emotions began to weave a new safety net that was kinder and more forgiving. It was the groundwork needed for my new life to unfold. Grudgingly, my guilt over not having been home at the time of the fire was tucked away, although always on call to take center stage at a moment's notice. Or it would descend unexpectedly, overwhelming the present moment.

During the first few years, I experienced panic attacks. I was at a printing shop one morning and suddenly felt like I could not breathe, like there was a brick on my chest. It came seemingly out of nowhere; I was not thinking about my children or the fire. If I worked long hours, or if a holiday, anniversary or birthday was approaching, I would become irritable or experience another anxiety attack. These experiences all fell away as I continued to heal over the years.

I spent over a decade in therapy with a psychiatrist and later a therapist. My healing work was geared toward helping me let go and let my new life unfold. In addition to talk therapy, I did meditation, yoga, and attended workshops about loss. I read everything I could find about loss and recovery, and studied and adopted philosophies that are still part of my life today. For many years, I vacillated between living in the questions of "Why them?" and "Why not me?" Eventually, the questions disappeared into the answers of my new life.

One writer suggested that children who die young are old souls that have come around for the last time. The thought resonated with me and, in a familiar sort of way, comforted. Slowly, I began to live life, finding meaning and joy again. I began to shift from having a life to being life. It was a subtle shift that was noticeable as I shared my old story less and less. I was making room for a new one to appear but did not know what it was yet.

I remember flying to the Bahamas from Miami one Mother's Day and every flight attendant on the plane saying "Happy Mother's Day" to my friend and me. My friend had never had children. We commiserated, laughed, and cried together. After all, we were headed to a nice weekend. I learned how to help myself navigate these times until I was able to fly solo many years later.

Today, I am grateful for being a mom, even if only for 10 years. That's something I could never have written four decades ago.

As the shock of my loss wore off and the repetitious monologue that was my story slowed down, a cold, barren landscape emerged. It was from the heart but not warm and fuzzy. It was a stark, fresh canvas for my new life. I somehow knew it was a turning point, but I was no artist or magician. I remember waking one morning and feeling as though something had lifted. I was not alone. It was the old anchor. Familiar. Loving. It was a coming home of sorts.

Helping Others with Loss

I saw a television show about pet grief about five years after the fire. The veterinary clinic offered free counseling services to clients who had lost pets. The irony was there was no free grief counseling for people who lost children. I decided to do something about it.

I wrote a small series of books about coping with loss, using my experiences combined with what experts said. Chapters included grief in the workplace, children and grief, death etiquette, using grief to grow, the funeral, and — finally — different losses and different issues.

One publisher suggested I parse the chapters into small books. He could not get through the first chapter of the manuscript — using grief to grow. It reminded him of the loss of his mother 10 years before, and he could not stop crying. I published the books myself, selling several thousand copies and using them as a basis for speaking nationally. The series became part of continuing education for the funeral industry. But I soon learned that a steady diet of talking about loss was tough.

Turning to Education

In the second decade after my loss, I moved back to New England to be near my aging parents. My dear father, a retired academic, suggested I complete my undergraduate studies to legitimize my books and work. He accompanied me to a Sunday afternoon tea for adult learners at a local college. I had been a music major 23 years earlier but knew my focus of study would be different this time around. I left the tea with a commitment to take four courses and a concentration in psychology and gerontology. At 43 years old, I began a new journey that changed my life forever.

Working in education was like a window of fresh air opening in my soul. I was challenged by the great thinkers, met people on new paths. Slowly, my story found peace and much needed rest in my heart. I did not realize it, but I started to envision my life differently. I started to form an idea of who I was and could be. I began to see a new pathway ahead, filled with options and opportunities. Teaching, research, a possible fellowship?

The result was three degrees in seven years. I pulled the curtain down on my grief books and work and focused on educational policy and disability. Both my parents had disabilities: My father had cerebral palsy and my mother had polio. They had successful lives that included four children, and it seemed like a safe place for me to use my talents.

I was 50 years old when I defended my doctoral thesis, 17 years after the fire. My focus was on the rights of people with developmental disabilities. My unspoken motivation in those days was to fix myself. Surviving my children came with an enduring guilt that is not really explainable using the written word. Somehow, if I just did enough or learned enough, I would make up for what happened.

Slowly, my education and therapy pried opened my heart. I began to get glimpses of what it meant to use my grief to grow. I began to reclaim the joy and meaning of being alive.

A New Career Unfolds

I became an assistant professor at the University of Vermont then moved to the 107th U.S. Congress as a fellow in disability policy and helped build a national nonprofit in Washington, D.C. My newfound purpose fueled my midlife work and contributed to improving the economic lives of people with disabilities. My early grief work informed my work in building disability-inclusive tax and financial education practices with community-based partners across the country. I built strong and enduring relationships with corporate and federal supporters.

The more I focused on service to others, the clearer my intention and passion became. I *did* indeed have something to live for. I found a new family through friends, work, and volunteering. Slowly, my grief softened into a compassion and a renewed trust in life.

My healing was noticeable in my work as I began a national dialogue one city at a time that guided community-based organizations to tap into the power of disability as part of their tax and diversity work. I learned that the views and biases people held about different "abilities" — whether physical, mental, emotional, or spiritual — were much like my early attitude about loss and required thoughtful and intentional dialogue, education, and patience.

I also became a mentor to many young colleagues and discovered a joy my tired heart had not known in a long time. I was growing a new life. My two dear sisters shared their kids — today, moms and dads themselves — with me. It was a generosity of heart I will never forget. Their grandchildren are also my grandchildren.

My healing was subtle. The more I let go, the more authentic and accessible I became as a human. I know my presence often holds space for others as a witness to the potential of our shared humanity. But being human comes with its baggage. When I am tired or feeling especially vulnerable, I recite the litany of *what if's* that are stored in the attic of my soul. A conversation might trigger these deeply buried treasures. It can happen when least expected, such as at a dinner party when friends share stories about their family and grandchildren.

Whenever the memory is triggered, I remember the love of my children. It is my North Star. I know the best etiquette for coping after all these years is still a loving hug, gentle smile, and knowing presence. And a continued sharing of lives, grandkids and all. It moves mountains.

Truth Chooses Life

It seems disingenuous to describe my life in a few thousand words, but maybe not. Just maybe it is enough for others to know that although the paradox of survivorship remains unimaginable, it is not.

I know that my story is universal, not special. Replace it with your own. Most of us live with the tension of a past and the hope for a better future. Many share with me that they could not imagine going on with their lives, let alone finding joy again, after a loss like mine. I agree. I did not think it was possible either in the early years.

However, in my seventh decade, I now know goodness prevails. I know life is bearable and forgivable. Even after the unimaginable loss of my family, it is my saving and enduring grace.

My dear father, now gone, always told me that my recovery was a choice. What mattered, he said, was my response, not the story. That has been the persistent theme in my life. I realize today that I grew into the truth of my life, despite my story. Replaced by a quiet peace, somehow my truth chose life.

It is both humbling and redemptive.

Johnette Hartnett's life and work dismantles the age-old paradox of healing. Now in retirement, she is available to share her journey for building a better future no matter one's ability or story.

Junkie

By Flavia Loreto

I was a junkie. There was a time in my life when every second of my day was focused on my drug. When I could not get to my drug, I went into severe withdrawal. During this time, I was not there for my kids. I was not there for my friends. I was not there for my job. I was not there for myself.

My drug was a man. I know now that this is called co-dependency, also known as "relationship addiction." People with co-dependency often form or maintain relationships that are one-sided, emotionally destructive, and abusive. My relationship had all those elements, but after several years of recovery, I'm proud to be able to share my story now that I am "addiction-free."

The man who became my husband came back into my life one day in February 2012 with an online message: "Hi, are you the girl I met at UCLA 30 years ago?" We had met very young in California and lost contact over the years. At the time I received his message, I was living in Germany. We began writing to each other daily. He was a lawyer and wrote in a way that totally captivated me. His messages quickly changed from simple friendship to passion.

Little by little, the messages became about control. He would give me tasks that I had to accomplish for him and if I didn't follow his orders, he would punish me by not texting, or blocking me for several days. It was an awful feeling. In a short time, all the messages and letters I received were manipulative and convinced me that I had no value without him.

He took pleasure in blaming me for breaking up our relationship when we were younger. He made me believe no one was interested in my photography. He told me people laughed and didn't take me seriously. When someone tells you these things day after day, you start believing they are true. I can see now how my soul, little by little, started to feel numb at the insults I received from him. During our seven-year relationship, there was not a single day when I didn't cry. I even tried to end my life and spent two weeks in a clinic.

Here's the irony. When I was with him, I felt good, no matter how he was talking to me or what he was doing to me. Just like when you take a drug. That's what these relationships do to you. You no longer understand what is right or wrong, real or fake.

Today, I can tell that I was trapped in co-dependency. I didn't know anything about it. How can someone become addicted to another person? How could this have happened to me? I didn't know where to look for help and no one was able to help me.

I always followed the rules and dedicated my life to my boys and my family. I had a good education and traveled. I had recently started working as a professional photographer. I loved to dance, play sports, be with friends, stay healthy and look good. There were no obvious reasons for me to feel insecure or have such low self-esteem and accept abusive treatment from a man.

Despite knowing how he was, I moved to the United States for him. I could not see the consequences. I dreamed that marriage would calm down the situation and make him more responsible and caring. We lived in San Francisco, where life was beautiful outside of our apartment but terrible in the privacy of our place. Co-dependency became domestic abuse with daily insults, name-calling, lies, constant outbursts, and physical abuse.

My youngest son joined me from Germany and in 2019, the three of us moved to Delaware, where my husband was from. I hoped that a life in Delaware would make him feel happier.

We initially didn't have jobs and stayed at his mother's home. Instead of one crazy person, now I had two. After three months, they threw me and my 10-year-old son out of the house for no reason. He put all my belongings in the garage and told me to look for another place and to pick up my things, asap.

I was a foreigner, new to Delaware, and didn't know anyone. My son had just started a new school. But I eventually realized that this was the only good thing my husband and his mother did for me. They set me free and forced me to leave a horrible and exhausting situation. This was the moment I finally started to become myself. When you're cornered by life, you either sink or swim. I decided to swim. I became strong and learned I did not need someone else to create my life.

I also learned how my background put me in such a vulnerable position. I am Italian, raised in Rome in a traditional family. My parents were focused on their children's physical and material needs but were not emotionally attentive. They were also very controlling, not allowing me to make any sort of decisions, not even the classes I could take at school. In their culture, parents expected their kids to respect and follow the adults' decisions. Children had to be always polite and silent. Girls did not have to be strong. Girls just needed to be pretty and follow their men.

This is how my mother and grandmothers grew up and what they accepted, knew, and shared with me. I don't want to blame them, because I know that they tried to do what they could and knew.

It is so amazing to me that now I can make my own decisions and create opportunities for my personal and professional life. But it has been a journey. I was so scared when I decided to buy my house after I left my husband. I felt like that little girl in Rome, afraid to take a step without her parents' approval. I was 50 but felt 15.

I did buy the house, and it was a good decision. I have learned that the ability and possibility to make choices for your life is an incredible privilege, but sometimes I still see myself as an insecure teenager. The positive thing is that now I am aware of it.

As to my addiction to my now ex-husband, I realize that I didn't have the knowledge of the problem. I felt very lonely and thought I was living an unhappy love, not a toxic relationship.

If I had had the means to defend myself and acknowledge it, I would never have fallen into such a relationship. Today it would not happen.

I have forgiven myself for being in that relationship. It has been harder to forgive that my son had to witness what was happening because of this man and because of my choices. This has made me feel very sad, but we have talked a lot, and we both see some positive aspects about what happened. I've learned there is always a positive aspect to whatever happens in life. Without this experience, I could never have started the deep introspective and spiritual work that has led me to be the happy and proud woman I am today.

Flavia Loreto is a photographer, specializing in portraiture as a way to explore the human condition and to capture the nuances of emotions and feelings.

Rebirthed

By Sierra RyanWallick

Sometimes life surprises you. My story begins 10 years ago. At first, I thought my life was ending; I didn't see that I was being rebirthed. That ending began a new way of doing things, pivoting my life onto a whole new train track, and taking me in a totally different direction with a lot of new baggage in my caboose.

It was the summer before my freshman year of high school. I was doing four sports at once: tennis, kenpo karate, ice skating, and volleyball. I was outside as much as possible, soaking in the sun and being as active a kid as you can be. But on June 10, 2012, I became very sick with a fever that wiped me of all energy. I never recovered.

I was diagnosed with Lyme disease, and my chronic illness journey began. My world effectively ended as I knew it, and a whole new paradigm began. My symptoms included brain fog, debilitating fatigue, skin issues, stomach problems, joint pain ... the list went on. And then there were the treatments. A PICC line surgically inserted into my arm that pumped meds directly to my heart and bandaging that caused what looked like chemical burn on my arm. The equivalent of a chemo treatment of medications that only made me sicker and gave me as many side effects as my normal symptoms. A medication that I took for two years that gave me severe depression and suicidal thoughts.

I went from testing into college level math in eighth grade to having to do my sophomore year of high school over two years instead of one. I would try reading one page of my textbook, and after 30 minutes, I would tell my mom I couldn't remember what I had read. I had wanted to become a veterinarian, but the science and math part of my brain had effectively turned off after contracting Lyme, and there was no way I would be able to go to veterinarian school. I didn't even think I would be able to graduate high school. It felt like all my dreams were going up in smoke, and I had lost my identity.

I felt so alone. Other high schoolers didn't understand what I was going through, and I had to grow up quickly since adult decisions about my health and my life suddenly confronted me at age 14. Several times, I thought about ending it all because there didn't seem to be a way out after years of treatments that didn't give me relief and only made my life more miserable. The one thing that kept me here was that suicide doesn't end the pain; it just passes it on, and I didn't want to pass the pain to my parents or my community.

My lifeline was my nonprofit called AutumnLeaf Fundraisers that I started when I was 10. Even through all of my health challenges, I was able to make an important difference in my community through the work I was doing. During my worst days, I could still knit items that my nonprofit sold and donated 100% of the money to a local cat rescue called Forgotten Cats. I was knitting up a storm because when my brain didn't work to do school, I could rest while knitting.

As an aside, I try to always call my health situation a health "challenge." Not a problem or an issue, because wording matters. Challenges are obstacles that can be overcome. Problems or issues are things that have to be solved, and health situations aren't easily solved, so challenge is the wording I choose.

Knowing I was making an impact kept me going. At one point, I thought about giving up my nonprofit because I wasn't able to keep up in school. But I realized that if I gave up my nonprofit, I wouldn't be making a difference anymore, and that was a huge part of what kept me going. Over the past 15 years, my nonprofit has raised over $100,000 for community nonprofits, engaged hundreds of volunteers, attended hundreds of events, volunteered thousands of hours, and affected more than 50,000 lives. All because I kept going and didn't give up.

At my high school graduation, I gave a speech called "I am a Survivor." It was a very emotional moment because I had made it. I had graduated, but it still wasn't easy. At every college I visited my senior year, I had an anxiety attack. I was scared that I wouldn't be able to go to college because of my health challenges. I was terrified that I would "fail" and have to drop out because of my health.

I decided to go to the University of Delaware, but first, I took a gap year to focus on developing the habits that would set me up for success. That was a defining year in building the foundation of habits I needed by focusing on what I knew was helpful for me instead of what others told me was best for me.

My strategy worked. During my freshman year, I helped co-found another nonprofit and served as the assistant director of a student-run organization. My sophomore year, I studied abroad in Germany and was accepted into the Clinton Global Initiative University. My junior year, I founded a social venture called UP Cycle Design and have grown it to a team of nine people today.

That social venture has been my dream organization to run because it is focused on my three passions: sustainability, mentoring, and philanthropy. We upcycle materials that would otherwise end up in landfills or our environment, donate to community causes from each product sold, and mentor our team to reach their full potential. In addition, we created and led a program for over 70 high schoolers called Level UP that teaches about entrepreneurship, design, and sustainability.

Today, I have a 4.0 GPA. I'm taking classes part-time while I work full-time on UP Cycle Design. I am still challenged daily by health issues, especially in 2022, when I had a health flare that forced me to pull back on all responsibilities and focus solely on my health. But the lessons I have learned from my health challenges have been a gift. That's right — it's hard to believe but so important that I'll say it again: *My health challenges have been a gift.*

These are the biggest lessons I have learned:.

- **How important it is to listen to your body.** Many times, I have listened to others and what they think is best for me. While it's good to listen to the advice and opinions of others, you need to make the final decision, consciously decide what advice you will follow, and then listen to your body. Listening to your body will help you determine whether your decision was the right choice for you and then be able to stay the course or pivot if needed.

- **Constantly pushing isn't a great idea.** I gave into the hustle culture mentality. Because of that, I lived 24/7 in the fight-or-flight adrenaline stress response state. It was my secret weapon in being hyper-productive even while struggling with intense health challenges. But that has taken an immense toll on my body, and I'm having to entirely rewire my body to try figuring out how to live outside of the stress response state.

- **Find what works for you.** I have tried countless treatments and activities over the years to help my mental and physical health while facing so many challenges. For a while, I even gave up trying new things because I felt so frustrated when yet another new thing didn't work out. But I've since learned that you can't give up hope. There is an endless number of new things you can try and new combinations to try them in. After more than 10 years of chronic illness, I recently found that watching Reiki videos before bed allows me to rest peacefully. This took me more than 10 years to discover, but it's something that is changing my life. It was only because I kept trying new things that I found that this works for me. Don't give up — keep trying until you find what works for you, and even then, keep trying new things, because you never know when something else will work even better.

I want to leave you with a poem I recently wrote. I hope it encourages you to see the challenges in your life as gifts and unfurl your wings that may be invisible to you now but are already there.

Unfurl
Let out your wings
Feel the air lift you
And rise
A
B
O
V
E

Sierra RyanWallick is a social entrepreneur who is passionate about "Catalyzing Pawsitive Change" through her social ventures, passion projects, and her YouTube channel.

Moments

By Kathy Palokoff

My dad and I are driving back down the New York Thruway on a road trip to take my little sister to college. I'm 23 and trying to figure out the world. "Dad, what do you think is the meaning of life?" I ask with all the innocence and bravado of a 20-something.

He looks at me like I am a bit crazy. This is a man who never got past seventh grade but always had a book in his hand. This is a man who once tried to stop his oil truck from rolling toward a group of kids with his bare hands. This is the man who would dance to Beethoven in the kitchen, cry during Red Skelton's "The Silent Spot," ask strangers what they paid for their house, and secretly fry his beloved garlic and onions whenever my mother left the house (and actually think she would not notice).

His eyes go back to the road, and he is silent for the next 10 minutes. Just when I think he is not going to answer, he says: "To be happy and try not to hurt people." I am disappointed. I had expected something way more cosmic. "Okay," I respond, and we go back to talking about the stock market.

It takes me 30 years to realize that his answer was profound and right. I learned an important life lesson from that moment: the power of simple truths.

***

I am at the Finger Lakes Grassroots Festival. My best friend, son, and grandchildren are all checking into the Airbnb for two days of music, dancing, and fun. I walk into my room, and there is a quilt on the bed. Jan has captured all our Best Friend Surprise Birthday Adventures in this beautiful piece of art. I can feel the love in every stitch. The tears begin to flow.

Jan has been my best friend for more than 50 years. I met her when I was a lonely ninth grader starting a new school. I had never met someone who was as funny, smart, and loving as she was. It was best friend at first sight. Years later, we started a tradition of taking each other every year on a surprise adventure for our birthdays. The birthday girl became the Birthday Queen.

We even have tie-dyed t-shirts we wear on these adventures. One says, "It's my best friend's birthday." The other says, "and I am the best friend." People come up to us to tell us about their best friends and birthdays. Costa Rica. Iceland, The Legendary Blues Cruise. Austin. Lilith Fair. Miami. Best Friends Animal Sanctuary. Las Vegas. Newport Folk Festival. Woodstock 50 years later. The list of places we have gone together goes on and on. People follow us on social media in anticipation of the surprise announcement of where we are.

There is a deceit factor to these adventures. False itineraries. Requests for passports when none are needed. Pretend exits from airports. The surprise is an important part of the event and takes some skillful planning. And there is also an embarrassment factor. Native Americans cooking fry bread and hunky Icelandic men in a hot spring singing "Happy birthday" in their language. Plane passengers joining pilots and flight attendants in rousing song. Shout-outs in every restaurant and tourist attraction visited.

But the true beauty of these trips is the time we get to spend with each other. Although we live in the same town, we actually don't do all that much together because of different commitments, interests, and personalities, so our best-friendness gets recharged intensely during these adventures when our total focus is on making each other happy. I learned an important life lesson from these moments: the power of a best friend.

***

I put my phone up to my husband's ear as Muddy Waters belts out "Baby, Please Don't Go." It's an ironic music choice since I'm actually encouraging him to go. I've asked the doctors to take him off the respirator after two weeks in the ICU. The tests show he is brain-dead, but part of me believes he is listening to Muddy as his breathing slows.

There are two things that Andy loves more than anything: the blues and his dog, Jambo. Jambo has been gone for a couple of years, but I can give him his beloved blues music during these final minutes.

When Andy used to come home from work, he had two rituals. He would sit down with Jambo and ask him about his day. "How was school? What did you learn? Did you have fun?" Jambo would look at him with those Golden Retriever eyes, and I swear the two of them were chatting. Then Andy would plug in for the rest of the evening, the blues music blasting so loud that I could hear it despite the Bose headphones resting on his head.

Andy didn't truly hear me a lot during our 20-year marriage. He had Asperger's, which now they say is part of the autism spectrum. "I love you as much as I can," he would say. "Let's call it 80 percent. I'm not sure if I really know what love feels like." I, on the other hand, believed in romance 100 percent. I love loyal and hard.

He was also a drug addict. Maybe he was self-medicating. Maybe it was the OCD that was part of his mental make-up. Coffee, salmon, dark chocolate, crack—when he tried something he liked, it was all he wanted. I don't know why he was an addict, but he finally kicked the habit after multiple rehabs and almost losing everything in his life, including me.

Five years clean and then he became addicted to oxycodone after a doctor prescribed it for shoulder pain, despite knowing Andy's drug struggles. An employer who allowed him to handle sharp and dirty metal without safety gloves plus his inability to feel pain from cuts, due to the oxycodone, resulted in the staph infection that took his life.

By that time, I understood powerlessness and detachment. I knew I could not do anything to change him. But that did not stop my anger at a very sweet, courageous, and troubled man who had my heart.

Now his breathing slows and stops. I have never seen anyone die before and the moment between when he is alive and becomes a shell, staggers me. I thought I was prepared. I am not. The nurse reaches out to comfort, but I rush from the room to my car and start howling like a wounded animal. Despite the hard times, all I am remembering is the joy I had with him. Hope is gone. I have lost my mate.

Then I take a deep breath and realize with surprise that the anger that has been my constant companion for so many years has disappeared. All the rejection, turmoil, and hurt does not matter. It has become the dust that will soon be my late husband. I learned an important life lesson from that moment: the power of forgiveness.

***

I'm on a Greyhound bus traveling home from West Virginia University for spring break, an eight-hour trip. Next to me sits an impeccably dressed old man with a spiffy fedora and bowtie. In contrast, I am wearing my typical hippie garb of a flowing skirt, beads, and T-shirt.

"Let me tell you a story," he says and starts talking about having a happy childhood and wanting to be a doctor when he grew up. How he had to flee Russia because they thought he was a spy. The sorrow of leaving his wife behind when the Berlin Wall went up. The years in a mental institution because his family wanted his money even though he was completely sane. The court case to free him. And as he talks, he repeatedly asks: "You don't believe me, do you?"

We exchange addresses before he gets off at his stop. That's what fellow travelers did back then. But he is right. I don't believe his story. Come on: Who goes through that in a lifetime? But it was entertaining.

Three weeks later, I get a large envelope in the mail. It contains documents validating everything he told me. It hurts my heart that I was so skeptical, and he was in such desperate need for someone to believe what had happened to him. I learned an important life lesson from that moment: the power of empathy.

***

I am watching thousands of egrets, anhingas, and herons roost on the trees behind my wildlife pond. The sun is a brilliant orange as it closes out another sunny, warm day in Florida. I am so content in this little house, a joyful retreat from the cold and snow of the North.

There is a knock on my door, and a delivery man presents me with two big boxes. One contains two dozen red roses; the other is filled with paper butterflies that fly through the air when I open it. I forgot that it's Valentine's Day. My husband, Dom, did not.

After Andy died, I had no desire to get remarried. It had been an exhausting and unbalanced relationship filled with worry and too much caregiving. The only one who had taken care of me was me. Now I was 60 years old and believed that my time for a happy marriage had expired. But I wanted to date and have some fun. That part of me had not expired.

So I turned to match.com and actually enjoyed it. I met Dom for coffee. He was a really sweet man but wanted something more serious than I did. Plus, his looks reminded me of my father. Big shoulders. Same nose. Smooth skin. Balding with hair trying to fill out the middle. Lovely smile. I had no interest in kissing my dad. We said goodbye, and he was disappointed that there was no second date on the calendar.

A year later, I had my fill of men. My last "relationship" had lasted four months, and not ended well. But before I committed to dating only me, I went back to look at some of the men I had left behind. I was finally crystal-clear about what I really wanted.

I wanted to be adored. I didn't care about money or looks. I didn't care about someone who dazzled me with their intellect. I wasn't looking for witty repartee. I wanted to be cherished.

Dom and I went on a second date, again for coffee. But this time it was at the public market. For two hours, we shopped. He held my bags, moved crowds out of the way, and had a smile and story for every vendor he met. They knew him and greeted him like an old friend. I felt protected and adored. For two hours, I was utterly cherished. And that first kiss? He was so *not* my dad.

Dom has not stopped cherishing me in the six years we have been together. You see, I have never lacked love in my life. Lots of it. Adoration? Not so much. It feels very different to me. Sweet. Fun. Poignant. Slightly uncomfortable. A tad embarrassing. Beautiful. He's a bit more into PDA than I am (never realized that I have a bit of a conservative streak), but when I watch his face light up from an unexpected kiss, the world melts away from me. I don't give a hoot what the world thinks about the gushy old folks.

I arrange the roses in a vase and text him a picture. He sends back one of him grinning with a thumbs-up. My sweet man remains working in gray, snowy Rochester while I snowbird without him in the house he bought for me four months into our relationship because he didn't want me to be cold. I learned an important life lesson from these moments: the power of being cherished.

***

I pick up the phone. It's my friend Dave. He's the husband of one of my closest women friends. In fact, I introduced them. But that's another story. "Margot's gone," he says.

I'm bewildered. I just saw her at book club three days ago, and she never mentioned a trip. "She passed away this afternoon. Her heart gave way from septic shock." He gives me some details, and we are both start sobbing. It is a moment, and over the months, the feeling of gut-wrenching loss will be repeated over and over again.

Grief apparently doesn't work on a timeline.

I have gone through the death of my parents and a husband. But this is the first loss of a friend. A woman friend who was like a sister to me. How do I go on without her? Who will I whine to about the little things in my life? Who will I share my most boring stories with?

Margot and I were supposed to grow old together. Margot was supposed to grow old with Dave. Now I look at a Facebook post he has put up five months after her death. It is my favorite picture of her; she's sitting out on some rocks with a big grin on her face. The tears start to flow again as I read the caption overlaying the photo: "My mind still talks to you. My heart still looks for you. My soul knows you are peace." I've learned another important lesson: the power and the pain of love.

***

A final thought about moments. I now understand that there are big moments, small moments, happy moments, sad moments. Some fly by without me even realizing that they were a moment. Some come with immediate lessons while others take a while to learn. Sometimes, I am in the moment. Other times, I am in distraction.

In the end, these moments are the gifts I get to share with myself and others. They are what powers my life.

Kathy Palokoff is the founder of goFirestarter, a book creation company for change makers; Virtual Human Solutions, an AI services provider; Confidence Redefined, a confidence and body positivity platform for women; and Kickstartabiz, a marketing and sales platform.

Fully Abled

By Lauren Foraker

On a wintery January day, I graduated from college with my bachelor's degree in communications. I was working part-time to support my goal of pursuing a master's degree, specializing in management and organizational leadership, while serving the local community through volunteer work. The plan was to study abroad in Ireland and Scotland — the lands of my heritage — post-graduation during the month of April while maintaining employment as a social media specialist with my alma mater, Wilmington University.

As I was preparing to leave the country, the invincibility of my youth as a 24-year-old seemingly expired on March 20, 2019. Perfectly ordinary and physically active, I arrived at the chiropractor's office several minutes before my appointment time. My visits to the practice were routine and designated for simple structural maintenance due to the wear-and-tear nature inflicts on the human body over time. Sitting in the waiting room, I heard my name called by a technician and followed her back to the therapeutics area before making my way to the treatment room.

After the approximate 15-minute delay, the chiropractor was ready to see me one last time before I was to fly "across the pond," 15 days from then. As we talked about our families and activity calendars, she asked me to lie on my back as she placed her hands on the back of my head and neck to maneuver me into position for an adjustment. In a fraction of a second, I felt a pop in the left side of my neck when she completed the rotation from left to right, causing an immediate burning and searing pain to creep up the back of my neck and head and extend across the left side of my face.

"Wow, that was different," I said, as I tried to figure out what had just happened to me.

"I know — that was a good one, wasn't it?" was her response, accompanied by recommendations to apply ice and heat as needed.

Walking out of the practice, I knew something was not right because I was seeing stars; however, I made my way home with the expectation that the sudden onset of nausea, dizziness, light sensitivity, and intense pain would cease. Unknowingly, this was the beginning of a 16-day fight for survival.

When I arrived home and told my family what had transpired, they advised me to stay in tune with my symptoms and suggested that rest be the priority for the remainder of the day. I took their advice, but over the next several days, my condition became drastically worse. The burning pain intensified, as did the nausea and dizziness, prompting me to stop eating. I experienced audio sensitivity and developed the most startling symptom of them all while sitting on my living room couch: spontaneous and aggressive Parkinson's-like (full-body) tremors.

With my entire body shaking in a rapid, swaying motion involuntarily, I could not eat or drink without creating a mess and required assistance from my parents and sister to walk from one side of the room to the other, because the tremors significantly affected my stride and balance. I called my primary care physician to schedule an emergency appointment to determine my next steps forward.

Her directives were to ground me from my flight and schedule medical tests with specialists. The list of potential diagnoses was short and uncertain because all the MRIs and additional test results were considered "normal" despite my frightening appearance. Throughout this process, I researched various diseases and conditions that could be associated with my symptoms, hoping I could assist my medical team in identifying the culprit.

On the morning of April 5, 2019, a terrifying symptom manifested itself as I awoke. I was tremoring so intensely that my head began to snap violently to the left, as if someone placed both hands on the sides of my head and began driving me into an invisible wall. Disturbed and deeply concerned, my family drove me to the hospital, where I was admitted to determine what this troubling and mysterious adversary was. When the on-call physician entered the room, his brown eyes seemed to grow so large it felt as if they would swallow me.

"What's going on with you?" he asked.

"I don't know, you tell me, doc," was my reply.

After we addressed the standard ER questions, I elaborated on my symptoms and the manipulative action that started this terrifying journey in the first place. I added that my research included strokes and questioned if it was possible that I could have sustained one, since tremors can be a rare symptom of such an event. He said, "Yes, you may have sustained a stroke." The doctor issued a series of protocols that led to bloodwork, extensive exams, and imaging.

What they found by the early morning hours on April 6 shocked us all: a 10-millimeter-long interior vertebral artery dissection (tear) on the left side of my neck at the cervical spine (C1 and C2 vertebrae). "If you had gotten on that plane, you wouldn't have walked off," remarked members of the medical staff, as they factored in the turbulence and cabin pressure that would have undoubtedly ruptured my artery mid-air, leading to internal bleed-out.

I was exhausted and unnerved, but thankful to have received a diagnosis and to be alive, despite being a dead woman walking.

I was released from the hospital with a soft neck brace and with a regimen of aspirin for the next eight weeks to prevent clotting, accompanied by instructions to keep my neck and head still to encourage healing. Even though my CTA results notified me that my vertebral artery had healed seamlessly eight weeks later, my chronic pain and debilitating tremors occurring 24 hours a day remained unexplained.

Now, four years after the incident that permanently disabled me and resulted in a traumatic brain injury, I have found hope and peace in a new normal, immersed in doctors' appointments, hypotheses, therapies, and medication, with the help of my current medical team, family, and faith in Jesus. My current accomplishments include becoming an International Maxwell Certified Expert and Chief Executive Officer of my own consulting firm, Leaderly Consulting Group, LLC, which specializes in DISC Behavioral Analysis, Leadership Development, Personal Growth, Communications, Dream-testing, and Intentional Living for adults and youth. I am also committed to completing my master's degree program, which feeds my soul as an avid collector of both knowledge and skill.

Currently, I have the privilege of serving as a volunteer board member and chair of media and press with the multi-state nonprofit Pursuit For Peace, whose mission is to bring joy to the most medically vulnerable children and their families in our local communities through partnerships with fellow businesses, government entities, and nonprofits.

My future plans include composing a memoir about my experience and life journey to provide hope to people, young in years or young in mind, reminding them that traumatic injuries, disabilities, and other obstacles do not define the status of your healing and success.

You are fully abled! I am living, breathing proof that there is a purpose and promise in the pain, and that your story does not belong to you. It is crafted through hardship to be an extraordinary blessing of encouragement to others as they overcome their own personal obstacles. My life's work is solely focused on adding value to others by enduring harshness in grace and standing firm in bravery, because we never walk or tremor alone.

Lauren Foraker is an internationally certified Maxwell Leadership Team Member. Serving as an expert in leadership, communication, and behavioral analysis, she cultivates intentional growth through Leaderly Consulting Group, LLC.

Growing Up Invisible

By Beatrice "Bebe" Ross Coker

I've seen quite a lot in my eight-plus decades of living on this Earth, but the very sad truth is that I was unseen by most people in America. I grew up invisible.

I came into the world with the onset of Social Security as a federal mandate to pay for retirement. My dad graduated from the HBCU Wilberforce College in Ohio with a major in math and minor in music and was an early employee of the Social Security Administration. In fact, he left us in Jacksonville, Florida, promising to send for us as soon as he got settled, but evidently "settling" back then was a little harder than expected.

My brother, sister, and I grew up in Jacksonville, with my mom at the helm of it all. Fortunately for us, she was an English and French teacher. My mom taught at home and on site, and over the years, her students were regular visitors in our home. I heard lots of time that she was one of the best.

Of course, schools back then were segregated by Jim Crow laws, so all I knew at my schools were Black teachers, classmates, principals, and other personnel. I never thought twice about being in school settings without whites. Our schools fulfilled the definition and purpose for being called schools, and we learned!

We were invisible to the so-called majority community, but very much evident in the "colored" community. I have tried to explain to folks who don't look like me what it was like growing up "invisible" to whites and very visible to the Coloreds, Negros, or whatever folks chose to call us. Our communities, while totally segregated, had every profession, institution, protection, and all the rules, regulations, churches, schools, stores, and health agencies needed. We had well-trained physicians and dentists; I never knew white physicians until after my college years and my move to the Philadelphia-Delaware area.

History fails to tell the truth about much of anything when it comes to African Americans on this side of the Atlantic.

Why is this important for me to share with you? Quite frankly, because in our community in Jacksonville, I was taught to define myself for myself and that the definitions of my personhood by others were of no consequence. Why? Because I was invisible to the eyes of my white brothers and sisters. You can't give definition to that which you don't see, don't know, and care little about.

Was our growing up fun? *Yes.* Was it beneficial? *Yes.* Was it God-fearing? *Yes.* Did it teach me the gift of forgiving others? *Yes, Yes,* and more *Yes!* In a true sense, growing up in the South in the 1930s and '40s was a time of horrendous racial discrimination. Yet, I was blessed with strength to endure and grow, patience to understand and wait, and the courage to be who I was by my definition and not live by/as what "others" believed me to be and wanted me to be. To those to whom I was visible, I am so to this day.

What I realize and understand now is that in the South, many believed what they were taught by people who feared what Blacks might do in retaliation for the evils done to them. Search the historical text, and you will see very little of revengeful battles. What you will see is a people who fought for this country in every battle abroad. Our presence in all ways is beyond apparent. And we continued to fight regardless of the racist laws, policies, and practices we were confronted with upon returning to this side of the Atlantic.

Take a good look at the 1963 March on Washington, where Dr. King's "I Have a Dream" speech made history. Present at that assembly in the Nation's Capital were thousands more than at the January 6, 2020, insurrection. *No* arrests. *No* problems. *No* physical protests. Just all people openly seeking fulfillment of "We the People" and that "Perfect Union."

Thanks be to God for His Amazing Grace.

Beatrice "Bebe" Ross Coker has been a leading civil rights and education advocate in Wilmington, DE for nearly 60 years. She is passionate about ensuring that all Delaware children have access to quality education. She's also a published poet and playwright.

Freedom

By Allison Garrett

I placed little value on my freedom, like the old saying, "You don't miss a good thing until it's gone." That's why it was so easy for me to trade freedom for prison, serving time in a maximum-security facility after being sentenced to seven years for a non-violent crime. I captured that period of my life in a journal, and my memories are as vivid as if they were occurring today. The difference is now I live my life in freedom.

Losing Freedom

I'm confined to prison walls I can see, the reality of man-made limitations I can measure. I'm engulfed in loneliness; indescribable loneliness. I've lost all control of my life, what fraction of it I still possess. I've been reduced to life's simplest form, sometimes being considered less than a person. Every day, I'm reminded that I've lost control over mere decisions like when to get up, when to take a shower, and for how long. I'm told when to go to meals and where to sit, and I no longer eat to enjoy but out of necessity. I can't decide when I may talk with someone or to whom, and uniformed officers control the volume and tone of my voice.

I'm in a place where I'm not allowed to make simple choices. I have to live by rules, Each day is the same as the day before; one in which everyone is the same. We dress alike, eat the same foods, and share the same misgivings. I'm in a place overpopulated with people who no longer hide behind emotions and failing expectations. I'm surrounded by hundreds who are bound by the same chains of unfulfilled goals and dissolving dreams.

I merely exist as a case — a blue file — and an assigned number. It doesn't matter if I don't know what to do. Someone will tell me. After all, I've proven to the world that I'm incapable of making it on my own. I had my chance. I gave it up. It was my foreseeable end.

I lie on my bottom bunk and stare at my surroundings: my cramped living quarters, pictures fixed to the cabinet with toothpaste, a bar of bright yellow state-issued hand soap that rests on a sanitary napkin wrapped in light pink as my soap dish. The cluttered stainless-steel table and stools hold borrowed books: *Chicken Soup for the Prisoner's Soul* and a Bible. My brown cardboard box with a lid is marked Allison Butler OL8397 and contains all I own — all someone else decided I could possess. Anything I can't fit into the box, I can't have.

I tremble with fear because I'm comfortable. My friends and family are disturbed by my cheery attitude and smile when I should be depressed at my destruction. I laugh (some of which is the best laughter I've ever experienced) when I should be crying at the devastation I've created for myself and my husband, family, and children.

My life has been greatly simplified. There are no people to impress, no one to lie to, no one to disappoint, and no struggle to be who I was expected to be. I'm free from temptations, selfishness, and the pressure to have what my neighbor has. Free from my condition of life, my holding pattern. Free from my mind, my fear of being exposed. Free to serve while serving time.

Free to tell the truth, feel the consequences, grow and heal slowly and permanently. Free to be well, whole, and responsible. Free to forget the past, forgive myself for my failures. Free to develop patience through

pain; to live in the reality of today, not yesterday or tomorrow. Free to develop a positive outcome; to know myself for me in spite of me; to be weak, and to spend time with the brokenhearted, the stripped, the beaten, and the abandoned. Free to learn true compassion.

Finding Freedom

When I first arrived, thoughts of what I had done and why I was here did not fully sink in. Admitting I was guilty and had a problem wasn't difficult. I had many hours each grueling day to think not only about what I had done, but why and to whom. I still had all my sick secrets and was in denial. Of course, I didn't think I was in denial. I just decided not to tell "them" my business.

Ms. D. didn't see it that way. "Ms. Butler…" started a long period of nonchalant tapping away at computer keys, snapping gum, and making no eye contact with me whatsoever. I had heard so many stories about this woman. A flashy dresser who found the greatest buys at the thrift shop and was known to be a real #$%&. She was said to be quick to judge, offering her raw opinion about who she thought you were and why you were here. She told one inmate that she would end up returning to prison for the same crime. She told another that she was a manipulator who only cared about herself. And she pointedly asked another, "You know you are a drug addict, right?"

What was she going to tell me without even having a conversation? "Obviously very intelligent. Your psychological test results show you are a person with no problems whatsoever. A perfect life. But we know that's not true, don't we? I mean, look at where you are. I suggest you are in denial, Ms. Butler, and if I were you…" She stared at me, took a long pause and with piercing eyes, stopped typing and popping her gum. "I would come down off that pedestal! Right?"

"Uh …, yeah," I answered. What else was I supposed to say? She was the professional. She continued to enter notes into the computer, did a spell-check, and dismissed me with "Send in my next victim!"

"Next victim," I yelled, as I passed the other inmates waiting in white plastic lawn chairs right outside her office. I couldn't help but shake my head and think that was how she viewed us. Victims. Why did what she said bother me? The feeling I got when I walked out of that office was all too familiar. Low and deep. Like I've been let down and discarded.

I didn't want to feel that way, but I had no control. This was the way I always felt. I wanted to fix it but didn't know how. I wanted her not to see me that way, the same way others did. Could I really fix me to be what everybody thought I should be? That was my moment of revelation. I cared more about how I looked to others with very little thought about who I really was. I didn't want to be a victim or on a pedestal. I just wanted a good life.

I wanted to be liked and appreciated. I desired to be loved. That night started the real journey: the soul-searching for what I had truly lost. Me. I lost who I was created to be. I had no appreciation for the life I was given. I had assembled pieces of the lives of others to make up this person who wasn't me. That night I began again from the inside out. Take me apart. Dig deep and rebuild. Rewrite my story.

Freedom is welcoming confinement between four walls in exchange for an escape plan from my self-imposed prison. Freedom is power — the power to change. The cost of my freedom was giving it up. Don't misunderstand. Just like most people, I wanted to be home and out of this physical prison. Yet, I recognized that without it, the process of the power to change would be hindered. Without this mandatory opportunity, there was no time for self-evaluation and no place to cover old wounds with immoral and criminal actions.

I would still be working hard at being "better than" instead of "better for." There would have been no real gratitude or reflection on what God's grace is like, no true appreciation for my life exactly as it is and understanding of how to cast off my cares. I couldn't love who God created me to be or see great opportunities from my past and my pain. I now had the time to focus on my salvation.

Embracing Freedom

This is more than just my story. It is an opportunity for you to let down your guard, be vulnerable, and allow yourself to sit for a moment and consider whether anything about this resonates with you. You may have never experienced a physical prison, but if you have ever felt judged, lost, wanting to be liked or loved, unhappy with your life's story, and — more importantly — living in a prison of your own making, this is for you. You have another opportunity to re-write your story. Baby steps, little by little. Not the one everyone says you should live, but the way you see for yourself.

Today, I am free not only from physical prison walls, but from the mental prison of my own making. If you are ready to break through what's blocking you, you not only can, *you will*. Connect yourself with other amazing women and share your story, too. We were created to connect with others and tell our stories to transcend them. It doesn't matter where you have been, what you have done, or what others think of you. You deserve to create a life you love.

Allison Garrett is a certified life coach and personality evaluator who is the creator of Prison Break Success System,© which shows women how to get out of their mental prison.

The Story of Littlebags

By Anna Welsh

Ever since I can remember, I was always creating something, whether it was cupcake toppers or personalized gift tags for birthday presents. I didn't ever just create one; I created hundreds and hundreds of them and sold them to family and friends. But I wanted real customers and an online store. I wanted the world to know about my products.

To support my drive, my parents purchased a laptop for me when I was 9 years old. I designed my own website and set up the backend payment and inventory system. This was the beginning of my entrepreneurial journey. I also began following brands on social media and dissected their mission, images, copy, and layout to better understand their brand image. I realized that maybe cupcake toppers were not going to be my best business idea.

During this time, I took handwork classes throughout the year and learned how to knit, crochet, felt, and sew. One summer when I was 12, I came home from camp and showed my mom some clutch bags I had created. She really liked them and took one with her when we went to Michigan to visit friends. While we were out shopping in the Detroit suburbs, a boutique owner complimented her on the bag, asked who made it, and was astounded when I told her I had and offered to sell them in her store. I thought she was just being nice because I was young, but I received a similar positive response from an employee at another nearby boutique.

My inspiration to take these compliments and turn them into a business was further nurtured when I took an entrepreneurship class for middle and high school students. It was a year-long program that encouraged me to find my passion and harness the skills to write a business plan. I soaked up all the knowledge and advice I received from the mentors. I learned about accounting, how to register a business, taxes, investing, insurance, and how to perfect my pitch. I went on to win the regional investor competition and competed at the national level in New York.

The real validation that I had created a product that people were interested in buying occurred when I was accepted into my first juried artisan show. The women running the show had no idea I was only in middle school. The event was in Philadelphia, and I was overwhelmed by the positive feedback I received from customers. They not only loved and bought the bags, but they were interested in supporting my sustainable and social impact missions. Littlebags by Anna, LLC was launched.

In the beginning, the demand was overwhelming. I thought I was a failure if I didn't have my hand in every single aspect of running my business. There were tears, but my mom and entire family were so supportive. She asked me a very good question: "Does Tory Burch make all of her bags, handle the marketing, update her website, and photograph all of her products?" I knew the answer was no and that gave me great comfort, realizing that I wasn't going to be alone on this journey. My mom was going to help me build a team that would allow me to achieve my dreams.

Now I hold monthly meetings to plan six months ahead. The Littlebags team discusses how each product has performed, revenue, success of events, introduction of new product lines like our wedding collection, expansion to corporate orders, migration of our website platform, and redesign of marketing materials. The list goes on and on.

Especially vital is knowing the cost of materials, labor, production, packaging, and mailing. I take the lead on researching suppliers to find the best quality for the price and also handle the online ordering. Market research, as well as regular events to test new products and pricing, also helps us make well-informed decisions. I especially like the creative aspects of developing new product lines: sorting through and pairing reclaimed fabric, designing the website, staging photographs, and creating the displays. I share ideas with my mom, and together we integrate them into the Littlebags brand.

Our sustainable and social missions are essential parts of Littlebags and who I am.

I am proud that my company aligns with the United Nation's goals for Earth and human wellness. Each of our bags is third-party certified to contain up to 96% recycled content. In our first five years, we have rescued 3,600+ pounds of fabric from entering a landfill.

In addition, 15 percent of the proceeds from each Littlebag nurtures the minds and bodies of children in need. We have donated almost $20,000 to support childhood literacy by buying new books that reflect the diversity of all children and communities, so these children can become readers, writers, and thinkers. We also contributed funds to feed children during the pandemic.

Not shabby for a little company. To quote Bill Drayton, founder of Ashoka and inventor of the term social entrepreneur, "The central challenge of our time is to make everyone a changemaker. To do that, you start young."

It's cool being out and about and seeing someone carrying one of my bags, knowing that a small piece of reclaimed fabric that would have ended up in a landfill has turned into a useful and beautiful accessory. It's seeing the wonder in a child's eyes when they pick up a new, quality book that opens their minds to a world of wonder and imagination.

Each day, I juggle going to school and running a company. Many people ask me how I do this, and quite honestly, I can't pinpoint my exact strategy, although having family by my side has proven to be essential. I can't stress enough that without the support of my family, my business would not be where it is today. If I have a huge test to study for or hours of homework ahead of me, my mom is there to handle correspondence, finalize a speech, or prepare fabric for the manufacturer. Sometimes, simply reading a motivational message is just what I need to get through the day — I am a huge lover of inspirational quotes.

When I was younger, I thought I wanted to become a classroom teacher. However, my entrepreneurial journey has shown me that I can be a teacher in many ways — to other aspiring young entrepreneurs, children in underserved communities, and the sustainable community to find solutions for textile waste.

Will I continue being a businesswoman as I head to college next year? Yes! There's still so much more work to accomplish. At the end of the day, it's heartwarming to know that I am a woman-owned business with a strong sustainable and social impact mission. A woman who consciously measures her environmental and social responsibility.

There's something very powerful in all of that.

Anna Welsh founded Littlebags by Anna in 2017 when she was 12 years old. Littlebags is a sustainable handbag company on a mission to nurture the planet and the next generation.

Writing Stories

By Taranna Tabassum Tiasha

I press the backspace key until the page turns as white as an empty snowland. Once again, I try to entangle the jumbled thoughts in my mind and attempt to remember the *Ah-ha* moment of my life that I am trying to capture for this book, but all I can remember are the *Oops* moments. This has been a regular thing ever since I've tried to shape my scattered thoughts into neat words.

I keep falling into the depths of despair because I am not able to reflect my mind in the blank space. Being in the development communications field, I rarely struggle to create the stories of people I meet. Yet, when it's time to share my own story, I'm stuck and disappointed in myself.

Part of the problem is that my mind is an avalanche of stories, and I can't pick one. Should I share my experience of developing stories about the indigenous youths in remote forests who dropped out of school because of poverty, yet kept moving forward to become environmental stewards? I have witnessed their courage and enthusiasm to transform their lives. Their zeal fills my heart with hope and gives me the opportunity to find the bright light of life.

Or should I talk about my experience at the coastal villages, which are paying the high price of climate change, even though they have not contributed to the disaster? How saline water intrusion has left them no choice but to leave their native grounds behind? How their watersheds have turned saltier than their tears? These real-life situations, shared by the coastal community, have had a profound impact on my life. I cannot tell my story by leaving them aside because they are part of my journey to become myself.

I stare at the sunset's fiery yet calm crimson tint blending into the darkness of the horizon. I stare at my reflection in the glass of the window and see the woman who has captured these stories in written and visual form. Then, eureka! I think I have found the *Ah-ha* moment to share: my place of power.

The answer has always close to me, and I didn't notice it. It's the urge of those bright minds to be seen and heard. It's the inspiration I get from listening to such diverse and wonderful journeys. I am and want to be their voice.

My *Ah-ha* moment has happened not once but multiple times. Whenever I have heard stories from the indigenous youths of the deep-green forests, the child brides from the drowning coast, or the abandoned grandma from the tiny hut with a sack as a roof, I have that moment. All these moments are precious to me because they made me count my blessings and realize who I am and what I want. And I know more moments are yet to come.

Hence, I take a step forward this time. I started filling my empty pages of white snowland with the gleaming colors of spring.

Taranna Tabassum (Tiasha) is a Research Assistant at the Center for Critical and Qualitative Studies (CQS) after completing her BSS in Media Studies & Journalism at the University of Liberal Arts, Bangladesh. She is passionate about her work as a development communication professional.

Searching for Home

By Sindy Rodriguez

As I sleep so peacefully in my bed, dreaming about Barbie dolls and McDonald's, I let my guard down and allow my body to relax. I peed my bed for what feels like the hundredth time. The cold feeling of those wet sheets wakes me up, and reality quickly sinks in. How am I going to explain this again? I can't confess that I slept so deeply because I was intoxicated with pure happiness of a life I wish I had, so I will do what I always do: lie, take the beating, and promise it won't happen again. But he knows it will.

Growing Up

My earliest memory of my mother was the way she smelled and the softness of her skin; she always left a hint of Maja-scented face powder in her wake. I wanted to touch and take in her aroma and found so much comfort in her arms.

But my father overshadowed this much-needed comfort. We lived a life filled with emotional and physical abuse. My father, who in his defense only had a fifth-grade education, lived by the philosophy of "if you don't put nothing in, you can't take nothing out" and "nothing is cheaper than free." He ran the home like a prison, demanding respect and perfection from babies. If we dared to act like the innocent children we were, there was hell to pay.

As a little girl, I sucked my thumb and peed the bed. The peeing the bed part was something my father could not accept. I remember waking up to find him seated next to me. He asked, "Did you pee your bed?" As I lay terrified in a puddle of piss, all I could do was lie, "No, Papi!" The ass-whipping and the destruction of my bed is a memory I still have a hard time shaking.

My mother told me how my siblings and I mastered the art of diving under the bed in precise order as we ran from him. We would roll back and forth from one end of the bed to the other, trying not to endure the pain of the broom he was attacking us with. He would eventually grow tired and tear the bed apart, mattress first, then box spring, leaving us nowhere to hide. My mom said we looked like a bunch of roaches fleeing for our lives, but she could not stop him.

We lived in New Castle, DE in a prominently white neighborhood, where people of color were not welcome. Although I do not specifically remember racism, we were forced to leave because we were not wanted there. We ended up moving to 4th Street on the west side of Wilmington, DE, on a block that consisted of Puerto Rican and African American families. It felt exactly like where we belonged. My mom immediately made friends with the neighbors and, with the advice of newfound friends, figured out how to receive state assistance in the form of food stamps and a monthly stipend.

She felt power from having this money and slowly gained confidence that my father could no longer control her the way he always had. She collected the money behind his back and began having her own affairs, just like my father. She would give her friends money, buy us nice clothes for school and food from McDonalds, and she absolutely made sure my father never saw the new clothes.

But he found out, and there were consequences to be paid. My parents were in the kitchen when I heard the yelling and saw her running. My father pulled the cooking pork shoulder out of the oven and threw it, hitting her on her back. I remember my mom being sad for days, but what we did not know was that she was planning her escape from the abuse. She waited for all of us to go to sleep and snuck out of the house, leaving behind my two sisters, my brother, and me. In the days to come, she came back for my brother and sister, who were not my father's biological children.

My father immediately carted my sister and me off to Philadelphia to live with his cousin and her family. They were complete strangers but happy to welcome us into their home. The woman who stepped in to become my guardian was beyond excited and told everyone that we were gifts. I know she was coming from a place of love and appreciation, but whenever I heard I was a gift, the only thing that translated to me was complete and utter rejection by my mom and dad.

When my father's ex-girlfriend found out my mom had left, she knocked on his door and made him an offer he could not refuse: In exchange for marriage, she would take care of his home and kids. This was all he needed to hear. They married immediately and began a life together with her three kids, two of whom were his biological children. My father was not in a rush to bring us home, although he did visit often and bring his bride with him. Finally, he decided to allow us to come home to Delaware for a visit. The visit went well, but then he took us back to Philadelphia.

At this point, I could not take the rejection anymore. My sister and I decided the only way out was to cry uncontrollably, which drove my cousin to pick up the phone and summon my father back to Philadelphia to get us. She was returning the gift. Finally, we were on our way home, but I soon realized that I had made a mistake. I wish I could figure out what my 10-year-old mind was thinking. Why did I come back to an abusive father and a mother replacement who only had love for her own children? I should have stayed in Philadelphia to avoid the next eight years that became filled with emotional, psychological, and physical abuse.

Quite simply, I lived in a house that was a home for everyone else but me. I was the punching bag, an outsider looking in and longing for that magical moment of feeling loved, accepted, and included. Without support and the courage to ask for help, I coasted in school and am still not sure how I kept getting passed to the next grade. I tried my best to hide my report cards from my father, who could not read, but my stepmother let him know that I was barely making it through. His response was always the same: "You are nothing but a dummy," with a firm slap across the face unless I was able to outrun him and make it outside, sometimes barefoot and in the snow.

On graduation day, I was overwhelmed with a feeling of accomplishment. I had earned my high school diploma despite everything. I don't remember exactly which family members attended the ceremony, but my father was busy working or with one of his girlfriends. When it was my turn to walk across the field and shake the principal's hand, no one clapped. I was humiliated. I tried to act as if nothing happened, but my sister threw the fact that nobody clapped in my face the moment she saw me. I no longer felt like I had accomplished something important. I was the unwanted stepchild whom no one loved or wanted, and my moment to shine was destroyed.

Becoming an Adult

After graduation, I immediately found a small apartment and moved out of the house that had only provided shelter. I began a journey to fill a lonely void, desperate for a sense of home that included love, acceptance, and family. Going through a childhood filled with disappointment, heartbreak, abuse, and loneliness had resulted in severe confidence issues. But I held onto the belief that love, family and a sense of belonging can conquer all.

I brought this hope to work. I was so excited and terrified at the same time about the opportunity to work for an established organization in the community that I knew and loved. The icing on the cake was that I would be right-hand person to a powerful Latina woman who led the organization. I remember a feeling of home and pride. What I did not prepare myself for was the jealousy, competition, backstabbing, personal attacks, and judgment.

During the early years, I allowed manipulation to control my existence and did everything I was told to do, even sending emails that were offensive to the receiver. One staff member tried to use one of those emails to get me fired. This employee even bragged about it and waited for my walk of shame out the door. Little did they know that the email was dictated by my boss.

Although my position within the organization appeared to have "power," I was slowly stripped of the confidence and energy I walked in with. It almost seemed that the goal was to tear me down to see if I would be able to endure the continued hostility. I could feel the laughing and backstabbing as I entered the building or exited the corner office. Instead of being part of change and a positive motivator to my peers within the organization, I regressed into my role as assistant, stopped caring about everything, and just survived.

My boss required that I be a mind reader and instinctively know how things should be done. If I dared to think otherwise, my common sense was challenged. The turning point was her screaming at me once again, as I sat in the chair in front of her desk All I could think was "Here we go again."

I wasn't focused on the issue, only her yelling. Like always, I did not react. I just waited patiently for the screaming to stop. What I did not realize was that her end goal was to see me broken in tears and begging for my job. Then, she looked me straight in the eye and said, "You don't cry because your mother left you!"

"Oh my god, I think that's true," I responded. "You are right. I don't cry because my mother left me." The tension in the room ceased.

The moment was therapeutic for me and powerful for her. Although she viciously brought truth to the surface, I believe she felt connected and appreciative of my attitude. The relationship shifted, and I became her trusted confidant and co-conspirator.

Those years felt like a game of survival to keep my job, my home, sustain a loveless marriage, and feed my two beautiful girls. Throughout this, I was still caught up in the dream of the perfect home that I could not find — a beautiful home filled with happiness, acceptance, and love. I believed others were better than me because their lives appeared perfect, filled with confidence, accomplishments, and support systems. Unfortunately, continuously not getting the home I so desperately needed at work or with my husband turned me into an angry, isolated person who exhaled ugly and pushed people away.

Coming Home

It took me years to realize that we are all broken in some way and on different journeys. My story does not make me less than; it makes me equal because we are all flawed humans. A painful reminder was when my mom passed. She yearned for her children's love and forgiveness. I was the only child at her funeral. I find solace in the knowledge that she knew I loved and forgave her.

Along the way, I met people who eventually became my mentors. They listened without judgment, asked thought-provoking questions, and reminded me that I, Sindy Rodriguez, have value; belong; and deserve to be included, applauded, and loved. They instilled in me the understanding that my journey is not dictated by someone else's opinion of who I am, what I am capable of, what choices I made, and where I was born. I alone determine what success looks like for me. I no longer chase a title to feel worthy of irrelevant people who don't matter.

Finally, I was able to move on from the organization I thought defined my worth and to a place of confidence. I developed a keen sense of awareness that it is a waste of time to drown in the things that hold me back. It took becoming bedridden with COVID for four weeks during the holiday season to finally connect all the dots and see that home was right in front of me the whole time.

My husband took care of me, my daughter checked my temperature every day and did the holiday shopping, and my dogs cuddled so tightly. In those moments, I realized my profound love for my son and for the father I had always pushed away.

I realized I could not take a second chance for granted.

This is what I have today: a second marriage rooted in friendship, a son I never knew I needed, two beautiful daughters, and four dogs that love me unconditionally. This is what I know today: I am no longer afraid of dreaming, allowing my heart to accept love, establishing boundaries, and believing in myself. As I continue on my journey, everything else is falling into place with a mindset of cherishing the good because being overconsumed with the bad leads to an ugly place that only hurts me.

And now I see the gifts given to me that I would never have seen as gifts. My loveless first marriage gave me two beautiful daughters. My mother's passing taught me the power of forgiveness. My father's philosophy of "if you don't put nothing in, you can't take nothing out," showed me the importance of hard work. The organization that tortured my soul provided the foundation for the professional I want to be and was the place where I met my husband, who gave me a son and became a much-needed father to my girls.

I have also gained the gift of self-awareness. Reflecting back, I realize that being vulnerable to love and acceptance has always been an uphill battle for me. I often worry that I will end up alone because of a defense mechanism that instinctively pushes people away or gives them "they are better than me" power that builds into resentment in me. These feelings have paralyzed my ability to connect, relax, and be seen for who I am. As a result, cultivating personal relationships has been torture.

Yet, there are people who are consistent in my life whom I reach out to when I need advice, a reality check, or a reminder that I am not that little girl whose father said, "You're nothing but a dummy." What I find fascinating is that people see a strength in me that I struggle to see for myself.

I know there are many things I should have done differently, but what I cannot do is relive or rewrite the past. Instead, I try to find strength in it and push forward. Sometimes, those dark shadows are way too heavy, and I find myself surrendering to them in moments of failure and disappointment. What I know is the clock is ticking. It feels like my kids are getting younger while I am aging at rocket speed. My insides are telling me to grab life by its horns and leave a footprint. I need to transition from admirer to admired, to be the topic of conversation, or the subject of my daughter's essays.

I cannot allow other people to paralyze my self-reliance and keep me in a state of irrelevancy. I know deep down there is confidence waiting to explode.

To those that continue to judge, dismiss, and roll their eyes when I speak or walk into a room, I wish you nothing but peace. As for me, I have forgiven myself and my parents and chase what fills my soul and focus on my path and mental well-being.

Lessons Learned

I leave you with this. You alone will define your self-worth, not the person who gets to stand at the podium, has a vast social media following, or believes they can inconvenience you by giving you their bags to carry. Just take it in stride, make a mental note, and know the day will come when they realize they sit on the toilet just like the rest of us. And if it takes too long because they are too busy cherishing the worshipping from paid employees and scared peers, move on.

Tear down that titanium wall that keeps getting in your way. Know you will have bad days, but when you get to the other side, you will be okay. Look within and accept that you are all you need to succeed. Do not allow gossip and other people's feelings, typically rooted in inaccuracies, to frame your thoughts. Stop letting people in power believe their mistakes are acceptable while yours are catastrophic, and that they are smart and you are dumb. Never let them dim your light or tell you can't because you can.

And please, find what home means to you. For me, it means the courage to allow myself to accept the feelings of comfort, acceptance, and security in who I am as a person; the knowledge that I do belong; and a structure where I have the honor of living with my family who loves me. That feeling is intoxicating and gives me the confidence to navigate life without feeling ashamed but filled with pride.

I am no longer searching. I am home.

Sindy Rodriguez loves the life she created and refuses to be defined by a resume. Sindy's greatest accomplishment is understanding the gift of love, self-reflection, and the power of vulnerability.

Racing Around

By Maureen McVail

I love going fast. For more than 20 years, racing cars was my avocation. Most people thought I was insane because I raced Porsches. This form of racing is called high-performance driving (for insurance purposes) instead of wheel-to-wheel or club racing. I'm passionate about every aspect of racing cars. I have driven and worked on several racecars. I have co-owned and managed a small but mighty racing team. I would still be racing today, but my reaction time is not sufficient.

Over the years, I was frequently asked how I got into racing. I wish I had a sexy answer, but I don't. I bought a used Porsche and instinctively knew that it belonged on the racetrack rather than in local traffic. My disclaimer here is that Porsche owners are typically thought of as snobs or highfalutin'. I was neither. I bought a used Porsche knowing it was meant for the track. My first racing experience was at Pocono Raceway. All I needed was my car, a helmet, shoe polish for car numbers, and a small overnight bag.

I will always remember leaving our home for my first event while my husband held our seven-month-old and three-year-old sons. I had been a stay-at-home mom for more than a year while he worked very long hours and enjoyed his golf hobby. He was an exceptional father, successful businessperson, and great provider. I felt I had earned a break, but I was criticized and shamed by him. Some of that was my own guilt.

The truth was that most people scoffed at my decision to do something for myself, but I was determined to follow my dream. An example of negative reactions to my pursuit of this non-traditional hobby was when I showed my Porsche to my Mommies and Me group. All of them owned minivans (so did we), but they were rather shocked and amazed when they saw my '84 Porsche Carrera in the garage. Their reactions were judgmental.

Ignoring the negative reactions, I took my first high-performance driver's education at Pocono Raceway. You have to work your way up from beginner to advanced. As I advanced, I had the extreme pleasure of driving on other major racetracks. My favorite is the iconic Watkin's Glen International Raceway in Upstate New York. (Driving clubs lease the tracks where there are professional races.)

By now, I have owned and raced numerous Porsches, and racing has been so exhilarating. People want to know how fast I've gone. That depends on whether you're talking about a straight line or cornering. The fastest I've gone is 145 mph. What's exciting is going into a corner at 60 plus miles an hour with one wheel lifting off the track.

Another question I heard was whether I was afraid of doing a dangerous thing as a mother of young children. My answer was always the same: It's much safer at the track because we have helmets and safety equipment and are all going one direction. It's odd that question is generally not asked of male race drivers who are fathers.

There were and still are few women involved in racing cars. I didn't notice sex or gender. I was focused on going faster and enjoying the thrill. I had mixed feelings about being called "one of the guys." It was meant as a compliment that I blended in with other drivers.

During my racing tenure, my vocation was at Drexel's Institute for Women's Health and Leadership (IWHL) for more than 16 years. At work events, I would frequently introduce myself as the special events manager earning money to support my avocation of racing cars. That would get quite the reaction. The executive director of IWHL frequently touted me as the in-house race car driver, which also received an astonished reaction. I became known as the race driver and was called fearless, confident, unique, gutsy, and bold (among other things).

My confidence and passion for this non-traditional pursuit resulted in becoming an advocate for women in motorsport. I co-founded Shift-Up, which is an initiative to accelerate the ambition of women and girls in all aspects of motorsport. Our key mantra is "If she can see it, she can be it." Thanks to a Great Dames introduction, I conducted a workshop for Girls Can Do Anything and presented these workshops to numerous clubs, schools, and groups. My objective is to share my passion for cars and motorsport, and I feel great satisfaction from empowering women and girls.

By the way, I still love going fast.

Maureen McVail had the pleasure of working at the Institute for Women's Health at Drexel for almost two decades. Her hobby is racing Porsches. She's a grateful member of the Dames.

The Pause

By Alice Palokoff

A number of years ago, I had an extraordinary encounter while I was working as a high school librarian in an urban setting. A student approached me as I was conferring with another teacher. "I need some books on the Holocaust for a report," she said.

I told her that the library had several books available. If she wanted to talk with a survivor, I would help her meet one. I told her that I also knew a number of survivors and had grown up with survivors' children born in Displaced Persons Camps at the end of World War II.

"Are you Jewish?" she asked.

" Yes," I responded.

Her face lit up, and she then remarked, "Oh, how I love the Holocaust."

I froze. I could not say a word. I was in shock. During the next few seconds, I wondered how to respond. I had never experienced such a comment. As an educator, I knew I needed to remain calm, keep my face neutral, and not show any anger.

So I paused.

"Oh, I didn't mean that," said the young woman, realizing how her words had sounded to me. "What I wanted to say was that it was good to learn that other people suffered in history, not only Black people."

The student left with many books, and I was left with many thoughts about this encounter. I was amazed at her having the courage to share her pain so candidly, and I felt so sad about that pain. I wondered how many young people and adults have a similar trauma. I began thinking of ways we can enable our young people to have more interactions on the personal level with people from all cultures to learn about other lives and histories.

Personally, it also reinforced a basic teaching of Judaism: Do not make a rash, quick judgement in anger.

I am truly grateful for the "power of the pause."

Alice Palokoff is a retired public and school librarian, and owner of her homebased business, Dor L'dor Judaic Books and Gifts, for 40 years in Rochester, New York.

Navigating My Life
Through Language

By Jah'Sima Cooper

Both of my parents are addicts. I was raised in a very affluent and predominantly Caucasian part of Chesapeake City, Maryland. Once my mother's addiction got very bad, we lost our place and were homeless for years, before moving to the east side of Wilmington, Delaware, where my mother is originally from.

Going from Chesapeake City to the east side was a huge culture shock because it was predominantly African American and very impoverished. My mom sent me from Bohemia Manor Middle School to Christiana High School. By the end of my first day, I knew I had no idea what I was doing. I sounded different than the other kids and didn't understand things they'd say. They kept asking me, "Why are you talking like that?" or "What, you tranna sound white?" or "You think you better than everybody?" In self-defense, I learned how to use slang, which came naturally.

But I had dreams of being in business, and I knew I couldn't speak that way in professional settings. I developed a very strong code switch, which is when a member of a group adjusts their language, syntax, grammatical structure, behavior, and appearance to fit in. At the time, I had no idea I switched back and forth from how I spoke in Maryland to the language of my school and neighborhood.

When we moved to Delaware, I started investing my time in business events and college preparatory programs. I joined TeenSHARP, a program whose mission is to increase underrepresented students' access to college and develop student-leaders who are successful, high-achieving, and reaching potential. They told me about the Great Dames Remarkable Youth Pitch Competition.

Once I realized what I signed up for, I felt a pit growing in my stomach. How could I, the daughter of two addicts, go on stage and speak to a room full of older white people who would probably care less about my struggles? How could I present an idea to affect change and improve the quality of life, based on something I've experienced in my life? And to top it all off, I only had a minute to pitch.

I went to one of my mentors, Ms. Tatianna, and told her I didn't think I could do it. She had never asked me if I wanted to do it. She told me that I had to do it, and she knew I was going to do very well. I instantly wanted to throw up. But she was absolutely right and gave me exactly what I needed to change my attitude. I practiced and practiced at TeenSHARP every day after school.

The day of the competition came, and I couldn't have felt more awful, even after having practice sessions with other girls and people from Great Dames. Everyone in the room looked the complete opposite of me. They were professional, dressed very nicely, and spoke better than I had ever. The only thing I could find to wear that night was my old homecoming dress and heels. The heels were so uncomfortable that I wobbled when I walked. The dress was so short I didn't even want to stand up.

Before I knew it, they had us lining up on the side of the stage. and then it was my turn. I don't remember what I said. I don't remember walking on stage or off. All I felt was mortified.

To my shock, I won second place.

When I got home, I was so excited to tell my mom, but she was high and on her way out the door. Instantly, I felt that pit coming back in my stomach, but this time, it was filled with anger. We argued, and she left. That's how it went around there. After the argument, I still didn't feel like she understood me. I definitely didn't understand her.

I went into my room, sat on my mattress, and started thinking. How could I walk into a room full of people who were much older and looked nothing like me, but still speak their language? They understood and heard me. But in my personal life, there was such a disconnect. I talked differently with friends and family, using slang, fewer and smaller words, and phrases like "you feel me" or "know what im saying" But there was some sort of friction when it came to expressing our perspectives to each other. There were always words used for lack of better words that caused a lot of cursing and, in turn, escalated the situation. My professional life took me away from how messed up my personal life was, but I couldn't get my personal life organized because I was using a different language.

Growing up with an addict father who was absent and an addict mother who was present felt exactly the same. I never had the proper guidance when it came to being able to articulate my feelings, voice my concerns, or navigate my personal life.

That changed when I moved in with two older white women, Wendy and Sandy. They became not only my mentors, confidants, and interpreters, but also the best examples of love personified.

I started watching the way they navigated their life and realized there was not much of a difference between the way they communicated in their business life versus the way they communicated in their personal life. They might have been more relaxed in their personal life, but when things got hectic, they reverted to the language they used in their professional life to get their point across clearly.

Little by little, I began to implement that communication style whenever I was faced with a tough personal situation. I would articulate how I felt just as if I was speaking to someone in my professional life, including the mannerisms. I'd find myself reconnected. It wasn't just speaking with a professional tone, but remaining calm, analyzing the situation, remembering who my audience was, and then responding.

All of those things have played such a tremendous role in who I've become today: a 20-year-old woman, single mother, and banker, living in my own apartment in Greenville, Delaware. I have tackled so many opportunities and built so many relationships by being able to apply this communication style to every part of my life. It is a power. That power has brought me here and given me the platform to share with you.

Jah'Sima Cooper is a 20-year-old mother and sister, who plans to be a defense attorney who strives to end the racial barriers and injustices in society.

It's Not About the Healed

By Haverly M. Erskine

No need for the white coats, the straps, the mice. I pictured a lot of mice. The mere mention of electric shock therapy as a possible treatment for my severe depression sent currents through my brain without any wires. It was an au naturel process. When my psychiatrist (who doubled as my therapist) suggested electroconvulsive therapy (ECT) in 2011, I felt like she reached the end of her rope in how to treat me. Wasn't it *my* job to reach the end of a rope? After two years of therapy and medication adjustments, it appeared that she felt more lost than I did. Didn't think that was possible. Either way, I wasn't ready for the electricity.

I told her I'd think about it, and I did — for a minute. I left her office, called my sister as soon as I got outside, and cried harder than I ever had before. There I was, 31 years old and the same weight I was when I was 14. I begged my savior of a sister to help me figure out what the hell was wrong with me. Begging my sister for help was not a new trend — I had done this for all things *big* in my life: my first speeding ticket, my chlamydia diagnosis, the first time I was fired from a job. My sister still has my back in life, and she's never judged me for losing my mind or not asking that guy to wear a condom.

Since 2009, when I began seeing this doctor, I held onto the smallest sliver of hope that I'd get better. Now the sliver felt like a pin prick. It was hard to maintain any sense of hope for recovery when my doctor played her last card. The ECT card.

I never saw that psychiatrist again. Not because I was angry at her, but because I needed to work with someone who might give me back some hope. I wanted to know what happened to the 20-something version of me who was a funny, intelligent, physically healthy, somewhat but not debilitatingly anxious, woman. How did she become this frame of a person who showered maybe once a week, barely got out of bed, considered a trip to the family room a success, dropped 25 pounds, never responded to calls or texts, binged on shows before binging shows was cool, and received but didn't use food stamps?

From 2009–2011, I tried to figure out how I fell so far. In therapy sessions. Restless days and nights in bed. When I crawled from my hole and sat on the couch. I tried to solve my puzzle. It's been 12 years since ECT was mentioned in 2011, and I'm still trying to piece together what caused my mental health breakdown.

What I know

For most of my life (I can't remember anything before the age of like, 5), I was your classic overachiever. I took elementary *tests* seriously, for the love of God. I *needed* to be the first one to earn the pencil box the teacher offered to the top student. I didn't want, I needed, straight A's in middle school and high school. I was class co-president, I joined every club I could possibly join, I played on three soccer teams (I was more social than competitive and captained the ones I could), I started working under the table when I was 13, and I worked at least 25 hours a week in high school while managing a social life, academic perfection, and my mother's severe mood changes (*if we could just blame everything on our parents...*). I won all sorts of awards, scholarships, and several other certificates that mean less now than they did then.

I never did what I did for accolades. In fact, I shied away from them.

A sense of humility was so important to me that I constantly put myself down. I still do.

I overachieved because I knew my capabilities, *and* I wanted my mom's approval.

Things didn't change in college. It was more of the same. I was annoyed when I got a B+ my first semester. It didn't happen again. I worked a ton, studied hard, joined a few clubs, and enjoyed a bit more freedom once I wasn't living with my mom. (Spoiler alert: My mom caused me a great deal of anxiety throughout my entire childhood and early adulthood.)

When I graduated from college in 2002, I moved back home. Remember the line from *Pretty Woman*? Big mistake. Big! Huge! I liken my anxiety to herpes simplex virus-1, the cold sore virus. Although dormant at times, it's always there and can easily be triggered by stress. If it shows itself, I want to hide from the world because it's really "fugly." I'd do anything to get rid of it.

Let me add some context. When I graduated, I got a job in Geneva, NY, which was just over an hour from my home. At this point, my father no longer had to pay child support. To stay in her townhome, my mom needed $400+ a month from another source. Thinking it was the selfless thing to do, I became that other source. I lived at home and commuted 70 minutes each way. I chose to make my job stressful because of my overachievement tendencies. I attended graduate school part-time at night in addition to traveling the country significantly for work. And because of a decision to live with a woman who made me crazy in a finished basement that reeked of mold, I had the "fugliest" anxiety every single day.

The truth is that my mom always causes me anxiety, and she always needs money. Everything in life is about her, and although I know how abusive her behavior is now, I didn't know any better growing up. I walk on eggshells when I'm in her company. I was fortunate growing up because I had two amazing grandparents who worked tirelessly to shield some of my mom's crazy from my sister and me. My grandmother did her best to take on the burdens my mom created, perhaps because she blamed herself for creating this monster. She took the majority of my mom's first punches. She gave my mom money when she could so we wouldn't have to hear my mom lose it when she "couldn't afford anything nice." She took the first of my mom's angry calls when "nothing ever goes right for me."

It pained me to watch my grandma absorb as much as my mom's crazy as she could. My mom made her stutter, and she'd wreak havoc on my grandparents' financial life. My grandma walked on eggshells as often as I did, and that pained me more than anything else because her wellbeing suffered. She didn't have to be the first line of defense, but she did it because she loved us. She died in 2007.

It's less so now that I'm older, but my childhood and early adulthood were plagued by anxiety. A pit in my stomach. Rapid heartbeat. Shortness of breath. Inability to relax. This is how my body responded every time the garage door went up when she came home from work, when her alarm went off, when I heard her coming down the stairs or walking toward my room. She'd rip through like a tornado, shredding anything my father gave us or any picture with him in it.

My anxiety paralyzed me when I had to ask if she could drive me to school, or pick up some milk, or tell her I spilled something on my new shirt. My mother's moods redefined unpredictability. Nothing scared me more than my mother in a foul mood. So yes, I feared every encounter. And oftentimes, no matter how well I did scrubbing the toilets, cleaning the borders, or winning academic awards, she was only proud of me in front of others. Behind closed doors, I was pretty certain she wished she never had me. In fact, she's said that more than once.

After four years, in 2006, I moved out. She called me selfish; I had anxiety. I packed anyway.

What I begin to uncover

I grew up with an overachievement disorder and a verbally abusive, narcissistic mother who most likely suffers from an undiagnosed mental health disorder. I grew up with a mother who was proud to have me as her daughter in the public eye, but privately wished I never existed. I was a burden on her life. As such, I grew up anxious as f***. My grandmother did her best to protect me, but that shield went to heaven in 2007.

I'm extremely hard on myself and have zero ability to accept a compliment if anyone tells me I'm doing well or look nice.

Logically, it would make sense for my breakdown to have happened in 2007. But it didn't happen until two years later. Why?

I recently began to read through some of the emails I exchanged from 2009–2011 with the psychiatrist who ultimately recommended ECT to help me figure out what happened. They're hard to read. It's a period of my life that's a blur now —because either I want to forget those days, or I legitimately can't remember.

On May 12, 2009, my email to the psychiatrist apologizes for missing my second appointment with her. I go on and on about how awful a person and patient I am, how I have terrible dreams and can never sleep. I beg her to not give up on me even though she only saw me once. I tell her I'll pay whatever the missed appointment fee is, and I'll do whatever I can to ensure that I make it to the next one.

This trend continues through multiple emails; I'm hit-and-miss on attending appointments. I eventually arrange to have a dear friend take me to and from my appointments — I knew I could no longer rely on myself.

I also find a series of emails from my mother that I forwarded to my psychiatrist with a note attached: "Can we discuss this tomorrow at my appointment? Once again my mother is tearing our family apart and making fun of my minor mental breakdowns."

I sent multiple versions of these emails in 2009, so the mental breakdowns I referred to must have happened before then, meaning I was already slipping before I started seeing someone professionally. It's all coming back to me.

It took me a few years, but in treatment, I also begin to understand the impact of my grandmother's death on my life. I saw my grandmother not just as a shield, but as a mother figure. She provided the love and protection that mothers are supposed to give their children. When I lost her, I lost so much more than my first line of defense against the person who robbed me of my peace; I lost a prime caregiver.

A mental breakdown doesn't happen overnight. It's like that "something is wrong with my car noise" that you pretend doesn't exist by increasing the volume on your radio: It's fine. Everything is fine. I kept my *radio volume* up for too long. I finally went in to check that engine light in May 2009. Throughout that year, it was ups and downs, trying to work my way through the issues with both talk therapy and medications.

In 2010, I still had some hope. I knew who I was becoming, I knew I didn't like her, but I also reflected on who I was. I noted things I looked forward to, which, to this day, still include my nieces and nephews. This is from December 2010.

There's really nothing new going on. I just feel so lost. I can't find a job. I can't find a purpose. But it's hard for me to get moving kick-butt style as I was just months ago because I'm back to a lack of energy again. I've lost a bit of my spirit. I can't find my happiness. And it's so hard for me to put myself out there, look for a job, launch my website, etc., when I have this dark cloud over me again.

Anyway, I'm looking forward to spending the holidays with my little nephews and niece. They really do cheer me up more than anything. And I have the most wonderful friends who care so genuinely. I am blessed for that.

My father is also sick, and no one can quite figure out what is going on. Although I maintain a great amount of faith, it is killing me to see him or hear him talk about what's going on with him. He doesn't ever complain, but nothing is worse than not being able to do anything about someone else's pain; not when I just want to make everyone feel better. That's the Haverly I know and love, that's what makes me me, and I can't be that person right now.

This email says a lot. My love for my nieces and nephews kept me going more than anything else. My father was the exact opposite of my mother (which is probably why they divorced when I was 2). He was very ill, but the cause was unknown, and his only concern was my health. Even though he lived hundreds of miles away for most of my life, my father was my sense of calm.

I felt lost in just about everything. Light came and went.

I uncover a new layer

The email chain with my psychiatrist that started in 2009 has been revealing and difficult to read. I'm glad I still have it. A mental breakdown is a product of years and years of unresolved pain and pent-up emotions. I had people in my life who belittled my emotions and those who only wanted to support my recovery. I was very self-aware of what was happening. I knew that I couldn't trust myself to make it to appointments, and I needed to ask for help. This was hard for me, and even though I struggled a ton, I wanted to get better.

I felt very lost and craved a sense of purpose. I was 30 years old, had no career although I had an excellent undergraduate and graduate school record, was unmarried with no children. In contrast, my 32-year-old sister had a great career, married the most wonderful man when she was 24, and had four beautiful children. I never envied my sister; I admired her (she's still my hero). I was extremely blessed to live vicariously through her.   There is nothing I love more than being an aunt, and I talk about those kids all the time. I'm quite sure they kept me alive. But I bring up the comparison because now that I'm a bit older, I look back and wonder if some of my unhappiness had anything to do with the standards that are so often set for women of that age. Career. Marriage. Children. Home. Since I was zero for four, was that part of the reason why I felt like such a failure?

I don't definitively know the answer to that, but I wish I explored it more at the time.

The year 2011 didn't start well. During a visit to see my sister and me in Rochester, NY, in January, my father met with the head of neurology at a local hospital. After 45 minutes with my father, the doctor asked my sister and me to join them. My father was diagnosed with amyotrophic lateral sclerosis (ALS) and was given one to three years to live. He was 64.

In the months after his diagnosis, I had several panic attacks, including one in the JetBlue terminal bathroom at JFK airport. I was en route to see my best friend in Naples, FL, in an attempt to get some *vitamin sea*. I missed my connecting flight, but eventually made it there. It was a wonderful one-week vacation. We stayed with her parents, who fed us well, made sure we went to the beach every day, and forced us to bed by 11 p.m. Even if I couldn't sleep, the routine was helpful.

Other than that wonderful week away, the rest of the year was painful. I broke up with the love of my life. We met pre-mental breakdown when I was more lively and ate real food. We were the love-at-first-sight couple, the annoying *soulmates*, each other's best friends, and we always had each other's backs. He wanted to stay with me through this tumultuous time. I insisted he deserved more because I could not envision myself getting better. We had what most people crave, what I still crave, and I let it go because I thought it was the selfless thing to do.

It doesn't take a genius to figure out why my psychiatrist ultimately recommended ECT. I was more depressed than ever. After two years of medicine roulette, nothing seemed to be working. I stopped looking forward to anything. I no longer wondered what was making my father ill. I pushed away the man who I had madly fallen in love with because I couldn't give him the love he deserved. In 2011, I was batting a thousand, and the only thing I could imagine taking away that awful anxious feeling was suicide. I had no interest in dying — I just didn't want to feel anxious and depressed anymore. I never attempted suicide, and I knew I never would, but the pain of depression and anxiety was that agonizing.

This is what I learned

Selflessness may seem like a noble character trait, but it's proved to be a double-edged sword. It has not served me well in how I chose to deal with my mom's inability to help herself or not trusting my soulmate's choice to stay together. I made the decisions to live at home for four years and break up with my boyfriend in 2011 because I was being "selfless," and both cost me tremendously.

We must be mindful of how generous we are with our selflessness. There's a sweet spot between selfishness and selflessness. Find it or we risk being awful to ourselves forever.

My father was one of the lucky ones. He lived for 10 more years, but they weren't easy years. He lost his ability to move his muscles, drive, swallow, and eventually, breathe. He never lost his ability to live, laugh, and love his children unconditionally, though. For as long as he could, he continued to sing "You Are My Sunshine" to me, just as he did my entire life. My father said goodbye in July 2021 while holding my hand. In every picture we took together (the ones my mom didn't tear up), we were always holding hands. To this day, I've never let go.

There are some things in life, both good and bad, we are never meant to let go of. Love and loss are two of them. Our life story is another. Look back, reflect, and learn.

I tried to work through my anger toward my mother's inability to help herself or think of anyone other than herself. I frequently became frustrated and anxious by her behavior and narcissistic mind. For most of my life, I tried to placate my anger because I considered anger to be a wasted emotion. Why waste anger on someone when I could use that part of myself to love someone who caused me joy? That anger turned inward and hurt me.

There is a good type of anger. It allows us to realize that some things are unforgiveable. At times, anger is the most honest emotion we feel about a situation.

When my psychiatrist suggested ECT, I knew I had to do better. My situation was dire. Although ECT is much different now than it was in the past, I still saw it as a "last-ditch effort."

After she made the suggestion, I moved in with my sister. The goal was to eat better, be more social (I'd be surrounded with my four little peanuts!), and eventually start working part-time. Although I stopped seeing that psychiatrist, I switched to a new one and began regularly seeing a new primary doctor.

We must always be our best advocates. I find this is especially true when dealing with mental health. We must do our research, decide for ourselves which treatment we find acceptable, and find the best support possible to continue recovery.

Dealing with a mental health issue will always be a part of my life. It requires constant attention, and I must participate in activities that help my well-being. These activities are not the same for everyone. Reading a book, eating a piece of candy, or being with my dog bring me joy. Laughter is my best medicine. I have regular medical check-ups with my doctor, and if needed, we adjust. I still get anxiety, but I don't put as much on my plate anymore, and I'm mindful of how often I interact with my mother. I'm a recovering overachiever. I'm not made for a 9–5 schedule, so I created a job that works for me. I cannot squeeze myself into a society in which I know I will fail.

If you're like me and have a mental health diagnosis, it will always be a part of where you've been and where you're going. It's much like an alcoholic who is 20 years sober. No matter how well we're getting on, we're always in recovery. Be mindful of triggers and remember there is no one-size-fits-all treatment.

I could end this piece here. I learned a lot in reflecting on how I got to my 2009 breakdown and 2011 ECT scare. But my biggest lesson came in 2012.

What happened next

After moving in with my sister in 2011 post-ECT recommendation, I slowly started to put the pieces of my life back together. In the fall of 2011,

I took a full-time job and was traveling again for work. I had some ups and downs, but overall, I was managing.

In May 2012, I was well enough to move back into my own apartment. I still spent a great deal of time at my sister's house, since her family gave me a sense of stability and unmatched happiness. Summer and sunshine were just around the corner.

So was pain.

In June 2012, my four-year-old nephew suffered a tragic accident in their swimming pool and died in my arms. I could not get to my darling to save him in time. Although he was resuscitated, too much brain damage occurred, and he was taken off life support. On that day — June 29, 2012 — our sky turned green, and the grass turned blue. My sister who had been my rock lost her son, and together, we lost our minds. And here, a new chapter begins.

At last

My college writing teacher always said that a good story doesn't have to involve death to be tragic. My story just happens to cross paths with it a few times. My mental health story will never be about how I healed; it will always be one of healing.

Healing. Hold on to whatever you can, do whatever it takes, and lean in. Just as light can't exist without dark, recovery does not exist without resiliency.

Haverly Erskine is the co-founder of Dreams from Drake, a nonprofit created in memory of her nephew, and a writer/editor at goFirestarter, a business dedicated to helping changemakers become authors.

Haitian Girl

By Bridget E. Kelly

As we enter the gates of the Salvation Army compound, she is there, swinging around one of the poles. She is in her own world. Lynn, the director of Haiti Family Initiative, steps out of our truck, and this young girl stops and squeals with delight. She limps over, barefoot on the hot stones. They embrace, and Lynn tells me she has been here for the last four years.

An orphan under her sisters' care, this girl looks to be about 14. She has some mental disabilities and is mute. She is missing her front tooth, drools, and walks with a pronounced limp and her left hand hanging down like a dead weight. She is dusty but not filthy. I can only assume that men have taken advantage of her. She is so vulnerable. In my own mind, I name her "Pitiful."

Pitiful has no boundaries. She stands next to me and slips her hand around my waist. She rests her head on my shoulder, and her hair brushes my cheek. I don't like this contact. It is too hot, and she is too dirty for my comfort. I try to squeeze away from her, but she tightens her grip. I am left with no other recourse but to use some force to free myself. "It's too hot," I announce to everyone in ear shot.

I try to justify my behavior. "She's pitiful, isn't she?" Lynn does not agree with me at all. "I've seen her grow up. I think she is precious." With that, Lynn gives her a full-body hug, and she squeals with delight. I walk away, ashamed of my callousness.

For the next few weeks, she is constantly at my side. She waits for me in the morning and joins us as I lead the women's empowerment group. She sits next to me on the bench and rests her head on my lap. When one of the translators barks at her to get off, she slithers down and leans on my legs. Sometimes, when she is resting against my leg, she takes her one good hand and rubs my ankles. Her dirty, dry hand feels like an exfoliation rag.

She looks up at me, and I playfully squirt her with my water spray bottle. She giggles with delight. She extends her hand to me. She wants me to squirt her again and again.

If I sit on any bench other than the one at the head of the classroom, she limps over and grabs my arm. With determination, she leads me back to the seat she thinks is rightfully mine, oblivious to other people and her surroundings. The women in my class ignore her, although sometimes they also bark. Sometimes she crawls away from this barking, but mostly she ignores them and slides into her own little world.

I discover that she loves to cut things with scissors, so I find scraps of paper and scissors and instruct her to cut. This occupies her time for a while. When she is finished, she wants me to inspect her cuttings.

Beth, a nurse, comes to our group to give a talk on birthing. My young shadow is resting quietly on Beth's feet. Midway during her presentation, Beth says Pitiful is in her way. Although I tell Beth to ignore her, she is too distracted and finds it hard to concentrate. I bring out the paper and scissors.

One morning, I realize that I haven't seen her yet. This is very unusual and worries me. She is always here with us.

"Has anyone seen her today?" I ask the translators.

"Who?" one of them replies.

Then I spot her. She is swinging around one of the poles. And I think to myself, "There's Precious."

Bridget Kelly is a retired public-school educator who now spends her time traveling around the world and looking for good stories.

Fear and the Solo Woman

By Sara Beth A.R. Kohut

It's hard to pinpoint where I picked up the belief that it was somehow improper or unsafe to do things on my own as a woman.

Perhaps it partially stems from my old-fashioned parents and their antiquated view that a *proper* young woman dare not venture out without a chaperone lest she find herself taken advantage of or falling subject to some kind of attack that might sully her reputation. Or perhaps it was a fear I picked up from modern news stories about women being attacked while out on their own (which is very much a valid concern). I hadn't realized how much I internalized these concepts and held myself back because of them — until I nearly passed up the opportunity of a lifetime simply because I had no one to accompany me.

In January 2001, I was a 24-year-old college graduate entering my last semester of law school. I had been a straitlaced, over-achieving student and was now in the homestretch of finishing my education, with the prospect of joining the *real world* and buckling down for a serious job looming ahead on the horizon. The upcoming summer would involve months of bar-review classes, culminating in sitting for the three-day Delaware bar exam at the end of July. I had a job lined up with a start day in September, which meant I had the month of August free —a last blast

131

of fun before embarking on serious adulthood.

As I thought about how to spend my August of freedom, one choice became the obvious answer: I wanted to travel abroad. I was both naïve and sheltered, having never traveled outside of the United States, but the lure of Europe was calling. Nearly every Saturday afternoon for years, I had watched Rick Steves share secrets from his "Europe Through the Back Door" book as he showed the great masterpieces of art, architecture, food, and culture on my local PBS station. After studying history and classics in college, I was haunted by dreams of seeing the great works of the western world and the ancient ruins of Italy and Greece.

There was just one wrinkle: I had no one to travel with me. I'd heard about plenty of people who backpacked across Europe, but I knew no one, certainly not a woman, who had done so alone. I was as single as a person can be, with not even a prospect of a boyfriend. I didn't have any good friends or close relatives who were in a position to take a trip like this. Any potential candidates I could think of were preoccupied with their own adventures in young adulthood, complete with full-time jobs, serious relationships, or young children. Even my fellow law-school classmates had other plans for the month. I could not possibly take such a trip on my own, could I?

The thought of traveling alone was terrifying. There were the obvious safety issues a solo woman would face. I'd already been living on heightened alert that last year of law school because a serial rapist had struck a victim in my building. There were also fears on a different level: I didn't speak any foreign languages or have a clue about how to handle foreign currency.

More significantly, I was an introvert and incredibly self-conscious about my alone-ness. During law school, I basically led a hermit lifestyle, rarely leaving my apartment except to attend classes or school events. Mostly, that was because I was extremely focused on academics and didn't have money to spend, but I also felt tremendous embarrassment about doing things on my own. When I did go out on my own, I felt like I practically wore a sign that said: "Caution! Single woman! She's all alone and has no one to do things with her! Isn't she sad and pathetic?"

As daunting as my fears were, though, the temptation of Europe was strong. I knew this August offered a trip that was a now-or-never moment that I *had* to seize. I kept researching and discovered that I could take a group tour and not be completely alone in discovering Europe; plus, as a bonus, all the details and planning of the itinerary and reserving hotel rooms would be handled by someone else. This helped to assuage my fears enough that I booked a bus trip that would visit 14 countries in 30 days.

When August rolled around, I nervously boarded my plane and landed in London. The first two days were on my own. I had prepared myself by reading all kinds of safety tips for the solo traveler, but I also knew that there was nothing I (or anyone else) could do to guarantee complete safety. I took my single self through the Tower of London and the British Museum, among other fantastic sites.

There were scary moments. I got lost several times, but I eventually found my way. My feet got so blistered and sore that I could barely walk, let alone run, from an unsafe situation. But it was all worth it because I was finally seeing, up close and in person, all these wonderful things I had read about or seen on television.

The third day was the beginning of my bus tour, and it started off seeming to confirm my self-consciousness about traveling solo. After breakfast in the hotel, the tour group gathered in the lobby to board our bus. As we introduced ourselves, one woman said she and her husband had noticed me at breakfast, eating all alone. They felt sorry for me and had contemplated whether to ask me to join them. Her words gave credence to my inner perturbation that the "Caution! Single Woman!" sign was every bit as real as I'd imagined.

But she quickly put me at ease, and I spent a lot of time with that couple on the trip, while also mixing with the other guests. Most of my companions were traveling in pairs (whether married couples, best friends, or parent and child), but there were a few other single travelers. Getting to know a group of total strangers who, over the course of 30 days, turned into friends was a wonderful experience.

In fact, it wasn't long before I came to appreciate being a single traveler. While I was aware that I was missing out on the opportunity to have someone close to share the experience with, I also knew I had a freedom my coupled-up fellow travelers lacked. I was free to pick and choose what I wanted to see and do. I ate what I wanted and when I wanted. I spent or held onto my money as I saw fit.

By the end of the trip, I had no regrets. I hadn't had to sacrifice any of my own choices on this momentous trip for the sake of a traveling partner.

Somewhere during that trip, I shed that "Caution! Single Woman!" sign that I'd imagined as a broadcast signal of my internal angst. Since then, I've never thought twice about traveling alone or going solo to a sit-down restaurant or the theater. In fact, I've come to relish my solo experiences, even after getting married and having children. Certainly, I enjoy family trips, but there is something about the freedom of being on a solo venture and choosing my own travel or culinary destiny that is both empowering and reinvigorating.

I've learned to feel perfectly comfortable in my own company, even if other people might feel uncomfortable by it (and I've had plenty of strangers in restaurants invite me, the solo diner, to join them). I would have missed some tremendous opportunities if I had let the lack of a companion stop me. Had I heeded the fear of doing things alone, I would have missed out on celebrating my 25th birthday on that August marathon bus trip in a Parisian bistro, enjoying champagne, escargot, and chocolate mousse. I would have missed the opportunity to visit Europe several more times and to sit in quiet contemplation at a Mexican pyramid thousands of years old.

That is not to say that traveling alone (or even with others) is without risks, safety or otherwise. I returned from that European bus trip just days before September 11, 2001. So much about how we travel, how Americans view the world, and how the rest of the world views us seemed to change overnight. Two decades later, gun violence, terrorist attacks, radicalism, and a global pandemic have further changed the stakes for traveling, not to mention that there are places in the world that are not safe for their own women citizens, let alone the unaccompanied woman traveler from America with the bold ideas that she can speak her mind or bare her hair, shoulders, and legs to the gaze of the world without fear of being beaten, raped, and/or killed.

While we can take precautions to address risks, there is only so much any of us can do to protect ourselves from the bad and scary things in this world. We have to be willing to push ourselves beyond the fear of these risks, as well as the imagined fears and stigmas our psyches pile on top of them, and not let them stop us from having experiences in the world that we deserve to have and that will enrich our lives. Had I not learned to trust myself and my own presence, my life would have been much smaller indeed.

Sara Beth Kohut is the principal attorney at Enduraylant Law, LLC, in Wilmington, Delaware. She writes and speaks on a variety of topics, including local history and privacy.

Financial Abuse is a Real Thing

By Suzanne Zorn

I always thought I could trust my husband of 25 years. Why should I have expected anything different? Over the course of our marriage, we did what many married folks do: split tasks so our lives ran smoothly.

I was a mother and the primary caregiver for our daughter, held a full-time high-level job, and took care of the house. My husband also had a high-level job, with a lot of travel, so I gave him a pass on household chores. He was responsible for taking out the trash and handling the financial aspects of our partnership. He enjoyed handling our finances and I didn't.

I should have been more aware. I didn't open the bank statements when they came in the mail — I didn't feel the need to, because I trusted him. I should have met with him periodically to review the family finances. We had discussed our common goals: work hard, save, and retire early, but I didn't know the goals had changed. They hadn't changed for me, and he never expressed any different ones.

I didn't know "the plan" had changed. My world came crashing down on December 2, 2009, when he dropped the bomb that he wanted a divorce. I was shocked, stunned, and speechless. Even as I write this, there is a pit in my stomach, remembering how I felt. My whole world collapsed. I felt the ground loosen underneath my feet. This was so unexpected.

We didn't fight, and the arguments in all the time we were together numbered five at most. I tried reasoning with him. What is wrong? How long have you felt this way? Let's go to counseling. I was met with a steely silence. He never explained himself. He had made up his mind.

I hardly slept that night. The next day, I went to work and told my officemate. She covered for me that whole week while I closed the door to my office and cried. When I came home that first day, he was still there and had moved into the basement. I tried talking to him to see if he would change his mind. He said from then on, he would only speak to me through his lawyer. I was hurt and confused.

Me, a divorcee? I received the official filing a few days later and realized I had better get used to the idea. This was not how my life was supposed to go. No one in my family had ever been divorced. What do I do now? What was happening? Why was he doing this to me? What do I do first? Obviously, I needed a lawyer.

Luckily, my place of work had a contract with a legal firm, although the first lawyer I contacted was so condescending and basically implied the divorce was my fault. At least I had the presence of mind to tell him we would not be working together. I called a female attorney, and we hit it off. She told me to collect the financial statements and then we would sit down and talk.

That evening, I went to the basement office where the documents were kept. All the statements, files, and checkbooks were gone. I didn't have account numbers or even know whom to contact at the financial firm. I was in trouble. But God, or my guardian angel, had a different plan. To this day, I still don't know why I searched for the backup key to his car. We kept the second set of keys in a metal box, and they were gone, too. I figured the documents I needed were in the trunk. I contacted the dealership and told them a made-up story about locking both sets of keys in the truck. They could make a duplicate key in a couple of days. I hoped my husband wouldn't empty out the trunk and move the documents in the meantime.

I picked up the key and waited for the right time to pop the trunk. He was still living in the basement, so I had to be careful because it would set off the car alarm. I waited until he was going to bed and turned on the TV to the highest volume — one of those WWII movies with bombs exploding.

There were four briefcases stuffed with financial papers. I took them to my office, the only secure place I knew, and started going through the documents. It turned out he had been cheating on me for years with several women. He wined and dined them using the proceeds from what was supposed to be our retirement nest egg.

I was fearful for my life if he found out I had the files and I realized I could not sleep in that house with him. For the next few nights, I stayed in a local hotel and alerted the staff, as well as my work security department, of the situation. I stayed late at work and used the conference room table to organize the papers, which were totally not organized. I had Post-It notes on the topics and would look at each piece of paper to try to figure out what it was and where it belonged.

I figured out that Lover #1 had received a car, a laptop, and a *building*. It turned out my husband had purchased an old pharmacy building in Bethlehem, Pennsylvania, worked with an architectural firm to completely refurbish it back to its original late 1800s glory, and then set her up with it as an art gallery and purchased several hundred pieces of art. Then he sold it to her for several hundred thousand dollars less than his investment, with the closing completed *the week before* he filed for divorce.

This was *so* planned. Looking further at the stack of papers, I found his to-do list. It listed how he was going to get rid of assets he had accumulated without my knowledge. At the end was "Big D" — his code name for divorce, and it was his plan to file once he completed his to-do list.

Some of the documents I found made no sense. One was a pamphlet from a township in Michigan that outlined when garbage pickup was and where the township administration building was located. I threw it in the trash, but something told me to fish it out. Why did he keep this? Why would he care when trash was picked up in West Olive, Michigan?

I logged into the county website and searched the property sales records under our last name. I typed in his girlfriend's name and got a hit. He never disclosed it during discovery as he was required to do: He lied and said he didn't own any property in Michigan. He purchased this with marital funds and put the property in her name to conceal the asset.

I knew I needed to prove this in court to expose him as a liar. The next morning, I called the company that had managed the transaction and told them a story about how my husband had bought this property for his sister (that would explain the different last name). I said now that it was tax time, I needed the documents and could they please send me copies. The following week, I received the sales agreement with a copy of the canceled check from our joint account. I now had the evidence of some his misdeeds.

The man I had trusted had already taken far more than his half out of the marital accounts and now he wanted half of what remained, including half the value of our home, my pension, my 401k, and my bank account! Meanwhile, he wanted to keep all of *his* pension and any monies he had already taken. He was so sinister that he even went after our daughter's bank account. She was a college student, and I had just put the next semester's tuition into her account for payment. He claimed I was *hiding* assets. He even claimed her Beanie Baby collection was *valuable* and he wanted half of its value.

He accused me of all sorts of things in court. His car was broken into during one of our court appearances. Someone used a crowbar to break into his trunk, and he accused me of breaking into the trunk of his car again, even though I had previously opened our marital asset with a key. I laughed hysterically in court and protested to the judge that I did no such thing. I thought the whole thing was ludicrous. To my utter surprise, the judge sentenced me to anger management classes. I thought about appealing this injustice but didn't have the money for the legal fees to fight it. I told my lawyer I would just go and do it. We both knew this was unjust and unfair, but I was so tired of fighting.

Each week was a different topic in anger management. Mostly, we discussed domestic abuse, since that is what got most of the women sent to the classes in the first place. We discussed men stealing money from their girlfriends and that's when I told my story of financial abuse. After the session, two women came up to me and said they *knew a guy* who could take care of my *problem*. I believed them. These were the kind of women who did *know a guy*. My answer to both was that I wasn't going to go to jail or hell. This man just wasn't worth it. Instead, I would continue to fight in court.

I've never tallied up how much I spent in legal fees. It's just way too depressing. Suffice it to say every bonus, raise, and spare dollar went into paying for my lawyer. I maxed out my all my credit cards. To save money, I did a lot of the research myself because I couldn't afford to pay my lawyer to do it. I would research where the money went and report summaries to her for court. I even hired a forensic accountant to confirm my summaries were correct.

Despite the proof I collected and the good legal arguments I had, the divorce proceedings took nine years — *yes, nine years* — to resolve. My husband refused to budge. He wanted it all. But I wasn't going to leave this marriage with nothing, so I fought him with everything I had. He totally underestimated me.

During those nine years, we spent more than 30 full days in court. I ended up filing an ethics complaint on the first judge, who made demeaning and derogatory comments to me about how I should have been more aware of the finances and that I "just wanted a pound of flesh." He said my ex just wanted to spend his remaining time "with the love of his life." Nah, I just wanted to come out of the divorce with a roof over my head and not have to work until I dropped dead, just so he could enjoy his new life with his new girlfriend and my money.

This took a huge toll on me. If it hadn't been for my job and our daughter, I think I would have been in deep trouble. I went to the gym as much as I could to get rid of the stress. I couldn't eat. I lost 25 pounds. I felt like it was killing me slowly.

I had had enough, and I put together what I thought was a decent settlement for our next court appearance. I had resigned myself that getting half of the original assets wasn't going to happen. We went to court, and I threw my proposal on the table. Without consulting his client, my husband's attorney said, "We'll take it." He had also had enough, or rather had made enough. My ex-husband was mad, but there was nothing he could do about it because the words had been spoken. It was over.

What did I learn from this ordeal? Never, ever, ever give up total financial control to *anyone*. I don't care how long you've been together or how much you trust them. As Ronald Reagan said: "Trust but verify." Every now and then, peruse the bank statements. Ensure the funds are still there. Have a conversation about the family finances. Make sure your goals as a couple are still aligned.

Make sure you have a bank account in *your name only,* or a credit card, *in your name only.* Why? Because if the inevitable happens, you have funds. You have a credit score. You can get a loan. You can rent an apartment. You have a name and a financial history. You exist. The one thing I did right, and it was completely by accident, was to retain a bank account and a 401k in my name and my name only. That was my only saving grace. Had all the money been put in the joint account, the loss could have been more, and the damage could have been much worse. I could have been left with nothing and no money to fight.

I didn't see it. I wasn't clued in. I was focused on all the other things on my plate and my daily to-do list. Until it was too late.

I learned the hard way that people change. You don't want to find out too late that you are the one holding the bag. It's a sad world when you can't trust the person you've decided to spend forever with, but it happens. Just make sure it doesn't happen to you.

Suzanne Zorn is a retired pharmaceutical project manager who enjoys trying new restaurants, international travel, and spending time with family. She also donates her free time to several local non-profits.

Stirred to Action

By Giftie Umo

I grew up in Nigeria as part of a closely-knit Christian family, made up of my parents and brother. We were not wealthy and lived in a community that was prone to flooding and crime. Nonetheless, happiness had the center stage in our home.

My father was a pastor, and my mother was an elder and midwife. The first time I saw a man supporting his wife to shine and live her passion was in our home. The patriarchal ego and rigid gender norms had no place in our house because anyone could be anything. Chores were not done only by the women because if Dad could do it, everyone else could, too, and there was no excuse why I could not do what boys could.

While my mom passionately pursued her nursing and midwifery career and ensured we stayed healthy, she also invested much of her time in rural medical outreach for women, especially pregnant and nursing mothers.

I was the oldest child and started middle school early. I was one of the youngest students in the classroom. My dad was very intentional about his children's education. No excuses were accepted for not doing schoolwork and receiving poor grades. His deliberate parenting style, which was very different from that of other parents in our community, communicated one thing: There is every reason to succeed.

I remember one beautiful sunny afternoon at the conference hall of the University of Calabar International Secondary School, where parents of 11th-grade students were to learn whether their children would be promoted to 12th grade. I sat with my classmates at the back of the hall. During the last school term, I had very poor grades in English and physics. Tightly crossing my fingers, I hoped that my Abasi (God in the Efik language) would have mercy on me, forgive my playful nature, and allow me to be promoted.

It was my teacher's turn to speak. I was sweating because I was not ready to listen to a sermon about why I had to play less and read more. My teacher said only 10 students on the list had above 8 A grades, and I was sure I was not one of the 10. As the names were called, I heard a loud baritone voice that screamed, "That's my daughter!"

My name was on the list. My father was so proud. His excitement changed everything for me then and still does today. I was now certain I would not be one of those girls pressured into getting married when I was not ready. Education meant everything to my father, especially girls' education, which was not a priority in my community.

Then my dad became very ill and died. My greatest advocate and cheerleader was gone. When cultural stereotypes gave me reasons not to believe in myself, he did. His death exposed me to cruelty and sexual assaults, but nothing could deter me from following through with all our beautiful plans.

Inspired by my mother's passion for her work as a midwife and my father's focus on my education, I wanted to become a voice for teenage girls and mothers in rural communities. I wanted to advocate for their well-being. Stirred to action, I ended my career in applied chemistry and founded Girls Leading Africa, which fully launched during the COVID-19 pandemic. It provides food and personal hygiene items to widows, young mothers, and households headed by single mothers and teenage girls.

The vision of Girls Leading Africa is to be a lens that diminishes stereotypes and prepares girls and young mothers for nation-building. Since our inception, Girls Leading Africa has trained more than 50 girls and young mothers in vocational and employable trades and has facilitated the return to school of many more girls. Our tagline continues to serve as our true North: "Reaching a Girl, Raising a Leader, Diminishing Stereotypes."

As a young woman mentoring other young women and girls, I have many hopes and dreams for the future. Most importantly, I want to continue to challenge conventional traditions and cultures that hold women and girls down, especially those in rural communities, by providing access to educational and economic opportunities for girls and young mothers to help them thrive while motivating girls to build their communities and their nation.

I hope to honor the examples my mother and father set and their love for me, my brother, and their Christian faith.

Giftie Umo is a social entrepreneur, founder, and executive director of Girls Leading Africa, a nonprofit organization that provides girls in rural Nigeria with the skills and resources they need to become leaders and challenge gender stereotypes.

Silent No More

By Robert Ford

All men
We are sons of mothers
Often brothers of sisters
Husbands of wives
And fathers of daughters

All too often
We, and that means me,
It means you
It means our fathers
It means our brothers
It means our sons

We bear witness, silently
Seeing and feeling the pain, maybe
Observing persistent inequalities, perhaps
Perceiving rinse-and-repeat indignities, possibly
And do we take action?
Not often enough

From our very first breath
Age-old signals and patterns surround us
Some subtle, many overt
Feeling hopeless and helpless
We often choose silence
Reinforcing the status quo

All too often making excuses
For ourselves and to ourselves
Quick to say that it's better than it was
Deep down, we know it's not enough

So what do we do?
We ask
We listen
We support
We hold space
We voice our truths

We show our mothers and our sisters
We show our wives and our partners
Yes, especially to our daughters
We show that they're not alone
Not us and them
But we, together

To our fathers and our brothers
And yes, especially to our sons
We show them a better way
Leading by example, we celebrate
That together, we move mountains
Not content with leveling the playing field
We commit to expanding it, for all of us

Robert Ford, a Great Dames male ally, is a consultant for nonprofit organizations, passionately working to empower youth, families, and entire communities to fulfil their potential.

My Twisting Road to True Purpose

By Wendy Battles

I've always wanted to be great at something, and it took me 54 years to figure out what that was. The journey to figuring out my true purpose has been like a road trip through my life:

There were periods of open road with smooth sailing ahead. There were times when I ran into slowdowns. Sometimes there was a serious detour — the type where you have to stop, reroute, and start again.

My journey started at a young age. I was 8 years old and taking beginner's modern dance at our local YWCA along with several of my friends. At the end of the term, the teacher pulled my mom aside and said, "Mrs. Battles, can I speak to you for a moment about Wendy? Wendy is such a lovely young lady, but she didn't master the basics of the class. I recommend that she repeats it."

I knew she was telling my mom something I didn't want to hear. I could just sense it. My mom told me what my teacher said, as gently as she could. I was devastated. I felt like I had failed. And I felt desperately left out, because all my friends were moving on to the next level.

My dance class experience was one of the first times I remember not being good at something. That's rough when you want to be *great* at something. I never did repeat the beginner's course. Reflecting back, I've come to see that small experience was a window into how I would deal with obstacles when things didn't go my way. Don't like the outcome? Then don't do it anymore. Quit.

We moved to Minnesota for my dad's new job when I was in the middle of ninth grade. I left all my friends behind in New Jersey. I felt depressed and sad. As a teenager, it felt like the world was ending. Fortunately, I found a bright spot. What ignited my 15-year-old spirit was an English class in which we had to write essays. Much to my surprise, I wrote an essay about a Shakespeare play and it won a prize at our end-of-year awards ceremony.

I was elated and felt I had finally found something that I was good at. Writing has proven to be an important part of my purpose in many ways. In high school, I learned I was great at writing reports and doing research. I honed my skills in college. Every single job I've had involved writing. To this day, I still love expository writing, and it's figured into my purpose.

Fast-forward to adulthood. I was pretty clueless in my 20s; I didn't really know what I was doing. Like many of my peers, I felt lost and was definitely suffering from impostor syndrome. I was in my 30s when I first started to tune into the idea of finding my life's purpose. Someone said to me, "Wendy, you have a great voice, you should do voiceovers." That's all it took. I took a class, make a demo tape, and literally started pitching myself to producers. I didn't exactly know what I was doing but gave myself the green light to keep moving forward — until the obstacles started showing up. Once again, I just decided this was too hard to do and stopped doing it. And then, of course, I felt like a failure. Interestingly, it was an important part of my journey, even though I couldn't see that at the time.

In my 40s, I was searching yet again. It was a really tough time in my life. I had a corporate job that didn't feed my soul, and my dad had passed away. I felt adrift and unhappy with my circumstances. I kept thinking that there's got to be more to life than what I was doing. I felt like something was missing and knew there was more for me, but had no idea what, so I hired a career coach and began looking into new possibilities.

I've always been interested in my health and had gone to nutritionists at different times in my life. The field of health really sparked my imagination, and I thought it might be something that I could do. I got a certificate at a nutrition school, quit my job, and become a health coach.

I didn't know anything about running a business. I didn't have a plan and only a few clients. It wasn't really the best idea, in hindsight, but I learned so much about myself. I learned how hard things can be and that you have to keep going. Unlike my previous experiences of quitting when it got tough, I made a go of it for two years. Ultimately, I realized that it wasn't my passion. It didn't bring me joy. It wasn't my true purpose. I stopped being a business owner and took a full-time job. The stability felt great.

Now I was in my 50s and feeling even more strongly that I needed to figure out what I was meant to do. It's interesting how things can conspire to support us when we have intention about something. I was asked to be on a panel at Yale University, to discuss career development and how we can create our own personal brand. I had done a lot of that when working independently as a health coach. As I refreshed my memory, I listened to a podcast about packaging one's true genius. The premise is there is something that we all shine at, and we just have to figure out what it is.

That captured my imagination. I ordered the workbook the host had written and started going through questions to gain clarity about what was most important to me to uncover the layers of my purpose. What do I love to do? What don't I like to do? What makes me happy? What energizes me? At the same time, I started to get really quiet and do things in silence. Cook in silence. Wash the dishes in silence. I tuned into all of the wisdom that was within me.

A theme emerged. When I was a health coach, I worked with women. In fact, I've always loved empowering women. I also realized, as a 50-something person who is aging and changing, I don't like the narrative. I don't like how women in our society are viewed, especially older women. I don't like the limiting narrative that the world has about what we're capable of doing as we get into our 60s and beyond. There's this narrative that we should hang everything up and just go relax, but not necessarily emerge as our best selves as we age.

I spent more time in meditation, being quiet, and asking myself deep questions. Then it came to me: I would create and host a podcast called "Reinvention Rebels." I felt so good once I had this epiphany — that I was meant to be a podcast host now. Did I know anything about podcasting? Absolutely not a thing! But I believe that when you get clear about your intentions and put them out to the world, things come into your space to support you to make it happen.

People started to help me. I mentioned it to a friend at work and he told me he could help edit the podcast. Then I was listening to a podcast one day, and the host talked about her program for helping women become podcast hosts. Sign me up. That was the next step.

Fast-forward to today. I am the successful host of a podcast ranked in the top 2% globally. Reinvention Rebels shares stories of 50- to 90-year-old brave and unapologetic women who have boldly reimagined their lives to live on purpose. I had finally found my own true purpose: to inspire women to see that anything is possible, no matter their age. Sharing the stories of older women who have reinvented themselves in the coolest and most remarkable ways inspires listeners about what's possible in their own lives.

All of those obstacles and detours in my life helped steer me to this place. Writing. Voiceovers. Starting a business. Health coaching. I have finally figured out what I'm great at. I have traveled a long journey and figured it out.

What I know for sure is that if *I* can figure it out, you can, too, in your own way and time. Always remember that you're never too old, and it's never too late to step into what you are meant to do and who you are meant to be. We all have a purpose and can figure it out. We have all the answers we seek within us. We can access deep wisdom and ease our journey if we're willing, ready, and open to listen.

Wendy Battles spreads joy as the host of a top 2% rated podcast, Reinvention Rebels. This pro-age rebel inspires unsure, 50+ women to boldly reinvent and find deeper purpose.

Making Connections:
Finding a Spiritual Community

By Geri Krolin-Taylor

I didn't realize it at the time but checking out a CD audio book from the library was a pivotal moment that would change my life in so many ways. The book was *Shepherds Abiding* by Jan Karon, and its red cover caught my eye as I searched for an audio book for my commute. *Shepherds Abiding* was part of a series about the fictional town of Mitford, North Carolina. I thought the book was very well written, and John McDonough, the narrator, was terrific. My husband and I started listening to the rest of the series.

The main character in the series is Father Tim, a balding, 60-something Episcopal priest. He lives with a dog he calls "as big as a Buick" and a red-headed boy named Dooley. The books tell the stories of the people in Mitford; how Fr. Tim found love with his neighbor Cynthia; and how they created a life full of grace, love, and family.

My husband and I had been married for a few years at that point and were living in New Jersey. Faith was important to both of us, but neither of us warmed to the other's religion. He was raised Methodist, and I was raised Catholic. We alternated attending each other's churches, one week

Catholic and the next Methodist.

Listening to these books was my first introduction to the Episcopal church. Karon wrote about the Episcopal service, how the church operates, and its hymns. In some ways, its service was very similar to Catholicism, such as genuflecting when entering a pew or receiving communion each week. The service was also similar to what my husband was used to with the Methodists.

The Episcopal religion was something my husband and I could both relate to, and we decided to attend services at a local church. The priest, who was a few years younger than us, was very welcoming. After attending services for a while, we met with him about joining the parish, which we did. After a year with the church, we decided to be formally received into the Episcopal faith. To prepare for this, we attended classes given by our priest. I had many questions, and he answered them all. I am so thankful for his guidance and the knowledge he shared with us. I still keep in touch with him and consider him a friend.

We didn't know it at the time, but we were looking for a community and found it in the Episcopal church. It was nice to talk about your faith with others, know they had similar beliefs, and that you were accepted by them. I became active in the church and joined the women's group. I was asked to be on the vestry (the lay leadership of the church) and enjoyed learning about how the church was run.

We moved to Delaware in 2014, and one of our priorities was finding an Episcopal church. We went "church shopping" for a few months before we found one we liked. We got involved in church groups and developed strong friendships. This helped us get acclimated to Delaware — we didn't know anyone there when we moved. Going to mass each Sunday morning gave structure to our weeks. Sometimes after mass, we would go out to lunch. Other times, we would just wander around town and people watch.

In 2017, we moved to our current home in Delaware. There was an

Episcopal church a few towns over that we had not tried during our church-shopping days because it was too far. It was much closer to our new home, so we went to their Saturday service. This was during COVID, and the Saturday mass was held in the parish hall instead of the chapel to allow people to spread out.

We felt a bit awkward because it was different from what we were used to. Fast-forward to COVID being over, and we went back to that Saturday evening mass, now held back in the chapel. The service reminded me of Catholic masses on Saturday evenings with my family. This priest was very welcoming to us newcomers.

At that time, we found out that I had endometrial cancer and would need surgery. After mass one Saturday, we asked the priest to pray for me. She barely knew us but spoke so thoughtfully that my husband and I had tears in our eyes. The following Monday, a parishioner delivered altar flowers to us. Soon after that, a prayer shawl from the church arrived in the mail. We were so moved by this — we were not even members of the parish yet.

At this time, I started asking my husband, "Which church would be a better support to you if something happened to me?" He said this church would because there were more avenues of support and opportunities for outreach. We started attending that church more frequently and formally joined it last year. It was one of the best things we have ever done, and it was all because of Jan Karon's book. As it turns out, we would soon need their support more than ever.

Last June, my husband had emergency open-heart surgery for an aortic aneurism and torn aorta. He was in surgery for nearly nine hours and in the cardiac ICU for seven days, with another seven days on the cardiac ward before being discharged. Since then, he has had three additional surgeries, and there could be more.

Throughout it all, the church has been a rock of support for us both. Priests visited my husband in the hospital and brought us communion.

I am convinced that being on prayer lists and all the prayers from the church helped with his recovery.

When my husband was discharged, the helping hands ministry set up a rotation of meals for us. Every day for almost two weeks, a meal would be delivered for our dinner. What a gift the meals were! I didn't always know what it would be, who would deliver it, or when, but I did know it would be brought with love and prayers. Not having to worry about what to cook gave me more time to spend with my husband and help him heal. For that, I am eternally grateful.

Today, we regularly attend the Saturday evening service. We volunteer with the church. We found a community that embraces us. The Episcopal church opened up a new world for us and made us stronger as a couple. It was something we did together: joining the church, learning about this religion, and talking more about our faith and beliefs.

When I think about all that happened in our life, I can trace so much of it back to an audio book checked out from the library. I have always wanted to thank Jan Karon for introducing us to the fictional world of Mitford and the impact she has had on our lives. It all started with one book.

Geri Krolin-Taylor retired early from her career in magazine publishing, spends much time volunteering, and is the president of the Friends of the Hockessin Library.

Saving Lives with My Daughter

By Carol Cunnningham

"This hospital desperately needs solar panels," said my 20-year-old daughter Kathryn when she arrived home after a summer volunteering in the Gambia, West Africa, in 2006. The Bwiam hospital had a generator for power, but it often broke down and fuel was expensive. Even when it was working, the hospital could only afford four to six hours of electricity per day.

My daughter witnessed the high human cost of lack of power: the death of a premature infant, postponed surgeries, and emergency blood donations because there was no refrigeration for a blood bank. I had never seen my daughter so passionate about a cause.

She presented me with a plan and budget that she had worked through with the CEO of the hospital. The plan was ambitious, but she was determined. I knew there were few large-scale solar panels in the Gambia at that time, and this project would be a significant challenge.

Kathryn asked me to connect with my friends while she prepared presentations and within a month, we had momentum. Together, we formed a board of directors and Power Up Gambia was formed. The next few months were a whirlwind. We contacted rotary clubs, found generous private donors, and scheduled visits to local schools. It felt as if our whole community was engaged.

There were plenty of hurdles and learning moments along the way. Who knew that our first installation would be set back by a family of rats chewing through the hospital's new wiring? We had supply chain issues long before those became an everyday phrase. Managing a passionate board, learning the nuances of international negotiations, and figuring out the fundamentals of solar hardware all proved challenging at times, but in the end, we overcame each one.

By 2008, Power Up Gambia had raised enough money for the hospital to build a pumping station for a reliable water supply. In 2009, Power Up Gambia had sufficient funds to install a solar power system with battery back-up to provide 24-hour electricity to the critical areas of the hospital.

With the solar power, the medical staff were able to expand their services, encourage more patients to seek care, and retain healthcare workers. As the patient level increased, so did the demand for electricity. In 2019, Power Up Gambia, with the help of the local community, raised the funds for an expanded system to cover the hospital's increased needs. Power Up Gambia also implemented "solar suitcases" for rural clinics and installed another solar power system for another large healthcare facility, Bansang Hospital.

I believe this joint experience had a positive impact on the world. When I reflect on what we have achieved, I believe it shows the power of youthful passion for a cause, a strong mother-daughter partnership, and community connectivity. It taught both of us important lessons about progress and problem-solving, but perhaps, most importantly, strengthened the bond between my daughter and me that will last forever.

Carol Cunningham was a cross cultural global leadership consultant. She is now retired and works with nonprofits in Philadelphia to improve the lives of women and children.

The Layers of Unfolding

By Gayle Dillman

I grew up, and I sense, like most of us, buying into the narrative that the best way to have a successful life, a rewarding journey, was to craft a linear one. A pretty straight line, as stable as possible, and reasonably predictable. A life of doing and achieving. Move forward, not sideways, and, undoubtedly, never backward.

Have you ever heard, "People make plans, and God laughs?" Well, my story (or this version of many different parts of my story) is one of starting over — the proverbial *reinventing* of myself. I have come to understand that the most significant part of moving through this journey of life is in the *being-ness* more than in the doing. It's a dance set to music heard at different tempos with various steps.

One of the most beautiful aspects of dance and music is that each person interprets it; there is no best, no right. It is your creation.

It has not been the most straightforward lesson to learn. There have been times I've wrestled with this *truth*, not wanting it to be this way. I was hoping that someone might *save* me. I am so grateful to have come through each chapter more fully than before.

This pivotal chapter in my story started about 12 years ago. I was faced with personal challenges; it became clear that I needed to figure out a new direction for myself and my life. The funny thing was that I had never thought of myself, perceived myself, as a creator. I was a mother, a wife, a daughter, a friend, and a million different labels. But not a creator. And yet, when I opened my eyes and saw that a new path was in front of me, suddenly, the 1,000-watt bulb went on, and it became clear that I had an opportunity to embrace this new way of looking at life and me.

I created a music events business, Gable Music Ventures. All I had was an idea and passion. I hardly even knew what I was supposed to *do*; I just knew that somehow I was supposed to be in the music industry. I started small with a business partner who saw my vision and took that first step. Our first shows were nothing short of disastrous, measured only by the degrees of how much money we lost. And yet, while I would have probably been taken down by the disappointing results at another point in my life, somehow, it continued to feel like this dance was the trajectory I was supposed to be on. I was learning that there is something to this *resilience* thing.

Like many startups, we hoped to get a break at some point, that we would find a winning formula for success. Mine came about two years after the launch of Gable. This winning formula was called the Ladybug Music Festival. My partner and I thought this would be a fun, one-off event.

Success was hardly front and center. I couldn't have understood then that Ladybug would dictate the direction of more than just my business for the next many years. Ladybug not only survived, it also blossomed into its own identity, power, and resonance, almost despite myself.

Fast-forward to 2019: The festival blew up to a two-day event with multiple locations, and things looked great. We all know what comes next. Two-plus years of retraction, we lost 75% of our business, and we were, like so many, simply trying to figure out any ways to stay alive.

How often can you reinvent yourself and your business? The answer is, *countless*.

Like so many business owners, I crawled out of my individual and collective societal hole to find a world that didn't resemble anything we had previously known or experienced. 2021 was not the year that would reinstate anything except for reinforcing the fact that nothing is certain, and change is inevitable. It's not always easy to embrace the truth. For me, it was another opportunity to see how important it is to deal with *what is* more than what we thought was *supposed* to happen.

A business partnership is undoubtedly like a marriage, and one needs to nurture it, recognize its complexities, and water it constantly. Although not too much — overhydration is as bad as dehydration. Balance is key.

By the end of 2021, my partnership had dissolved, and as 2022 loomed, I *knew* that I needed a new label for myself. I needed a new concept if I was going to continue. Another reinvention and another re-set were required. Get up (again), *Gayle; take back your life (again!) and your business ... and become your best champion.*

I listened. And that is precisely what I did. 2022 was a year that required the next reinvention, and the vast difference this time was that I understood, on a whole other level, that this one was *really* up to me. No business partner, just myself. Well, that is not entirely true. Any strong business takes a village. And mine is a dynamic team of business associates and a couple of close friends who have helped me strategize, hold to our vision, and make decisions that will secure the foundation of Gable and Ladybug (and Gayle!) for the future.

I am a huge believer in staying open and not contracting, especially at those very times when we might have that urge to go back to bed and crawl under the covers. It's essential to be reminded — and to remind ourselves — that possibilities and magic are often right there, just around the corner.

Gayle Dillman is the founder and CEO of Gable Music Ventures, LLC and creator of The Lady bug Music Festival.

Drumbeats: Remembering

By Karen Smith

Year 1: Foggy Father Year

Can't see much ... feel more, though ... there's some kind of strength around ... nurturing begins ... you are convinced I am the last ...

Year 2: Shift Year

Major loss of your queen, Marie ... the back of your heart is empty when you pick me up ... I feel your pain ... I cry for you when you can't ...

Year 3: I am Growing

Little less Foggy Father ... lap and nap times are my favorite ... I can walk, too ... I can look out the window for your return ... you make me laugh ...

Years 4–5: My Favorite Comfort

You are not around much, but my big red-and-white stuffed dog, Pierre, with his red tam, makes my days and night secure, and I love him ...

Year 6: No More Kindergarten

No more half days ... no more Ignatz and Krazy Kat Cartoons ... homework ... readin' ritin' rithmetic ... Pierre losing more of his stuffing daily ...

Year 7: Big Loud Truck Goes through the Block

My silence seems permanent ... Pierre losing more stuffing ... I lose my security ... I lose my love ... my suffering in silence becomes more pronounced ... don't want another stuffed animal again ...

Year 8: I am Different

I like what my brothers like ... cars, trucks, trains, action figures ... you notice my lesser interest in those specific gender things ...

Years 9 – 10: I Love Music like You

I love banging on things to make beats ... want a drum set ... Mom rules ... nope, an Easy Bake Oven appears ... maybe used once ... I didn't like Santa. ..

Year 11: You are Santa

You gave me what I wanted ... trucks, trains, G.I. Joe ... a boy's bike ... you are listening ... Mom argued but you listened ... but to keep peace, a grand piano appears as a compromise for these actions ... I must learn to play ... like a girl ... to keep peace ... I went to lessons only...

Year 12: Trips to Madison Square Garden

Basketball was your mistress ... we screamed from the stands ... you ran down the big court with your whistle, black-and-white striped shirt and black pants ... I loved popcorn and soda ... and loved seeing you do what you do, what you loved ... you also loved making us happy ... you worked day and night providing ... seven days a week and on top of that ... you made a special trip to MSG with the first cousins to see the Jackson Five concert ... Mark, Rodney, Candace, Crystal, , and me ... it was loud and exciting ... didn't know it was going to be the last outing ...

Year 13: The Last Supper

Who said 13 was unlucky? Foggy returns ... I am eating at the kitchen table ... rushing my dinner ... wanting to get out before it gets dark ... school night of September 27 ... you sat down in a white tee and dress pants ...talking to your queen ... I am too busy watching the clock ... I have at least one hour to hang out on my neighbor and friend Cornelius's stoop ... the conversation was blurry ... you might have tried to engage with me

... I was racing against my own time ... so were you ... I never saw your face at the table ... "Can I be excused? I finished all my food." "Yes," replied the queen ... "In before dark"... could not get out fast enough ... learning to play trumpet with Corny ... he was good and still a student ... we were on his stoop with two mouthpieces ... I didn't have the wind ... but the determination ... it did make me light-headed, too ...

The sun sets so beautiful in the fall ... and it was no different that evening ... Honk on the horn ... I finally look up ... you wave ... we wave back ... and you drive off ... sleep is interrupted by the doorbell in the middle of the darkness... Mumbles and then screams... "Your father is in the hospital!" ... time moves so fast now ... massive heart attack on the steps of 79th Precinct ... you never made it to that meeting ... no more sleeping ... no more security ... no peaceful night ... my world and perspectives changed forever ... I still see you in my day and night dreams ... Halsey Street ... the stoop ... the Brown Bomber (your last car) and your face ...

Year 61: My Inner Child is Forever 13

'Til death do us part ... continue to rest in power ... Robert Arlington Smith, Sr., April 21, 1916–Sept 27, 1973 ... by Child 8 ...

Karen L Smith is a percussionist, playwright and published author in two anthologies, 8:46 a tribute to George Floyd and Philly Jawns: For Women Revisited, A Tribute to Nina Simone. Possible is Possible.

Nuggets from a Seasoned Woman

By Patricia Russell

I grew up in a two-parent household in the heart of North Philadelphia in the mid-1950s. It was quite natural for everyone to look out for each other. Nobody was homeless. Everyone could correct a child without consequences. You helped your neighbor. It wasn't unusual for someone in your neighborhood to knock on the door to see if you had a half a cup of sugar to bake a cake. When someone passed away, a wreath would be placed on the door of their family's home and strangers would come by and offer condolences or bring some food to the family.

These were natural and daily interactions in our community that we simply don't see today. I didn't realize the impact and influence that strong community had on things that I value.

Another major impact was that my mother contracted tuberculosis and was sent away to a sanatorium for several years. I was the youngest left at home with my six older siblings. My three younger siblings were sent to other family members or friends during that time. I felt like I had too many bosses and missed my mother but didn't know how to express it.

During the summer months, the younger children went to a small town in North Carolina where my paternal grandmother lived. She and I didn't get along very well. I felt like I was in the way, and my natural curiosity seemed to anger her. When I would ask a question, I got either a short, curt answer or a spanking with a switch from a nearby tree. She wasn't equipped with gentleness and the ability to resolve problems tenderly, but I knew none of that as a little girl. I just thought she was harsh and unreasonable.

As I grew, I realized that I'm not a person who blindly follows anything or anybody without some degree of reason or logic. I remember hearing my grandfather talking about me as having a "free spirit." I didn't really know what that meant but thought of a bird, flying without entanglements or boundaries, but with a destination in mind. I tried to use that analogy to my advantage and would not be confined to the status quo.

Growing up, it never occurred to me that I would someday be a leader. It's nothing that I ever sought to be, but I've learned that your gifts will make room for you, even when you didn't know you had a gift. I've also learned other things on my road to maturity — what I think of as nuggets from a seasoned woman. I'd like to share a few with you.

- You cannot change another human's behavior. People do not change for the better because they should or because you want them to. They only do better when they are motivated to do so, whether through inspiration from others, severe consequences, illness, or someone showing them a different option. You can only change yourself, and your reactions and approaches to situations.
- If you don't know where you want to go, any road will take you. Therefore, establish principles, values, boundaries, or standards for your way of showing up in life.
- To accomplish your goals, you can remain respectful and kind, but firm. Stand in your own truth, even when you must stand alone.
- Forgiveness does not always mean restoration. It is important

for your own growth and development to learn to honestly forgive people for the wrongs they have done. I have learned that forgiveness means remembering without anger. Each situation is different, and sometimes forgiveness does mean restoration.

- Take responsibility for your contribution to the conundrums in your life. Own your own stuff, even if it means you recognize something as subtle as perhaps you allowed the crazy to continue for too long. It is always easy to blame the other person, but self-examination and looking inward is a very healthy exercise.

- Recognize your vulnerabilities and resist putting yourself in compromising situations. If you don't have a family, friends, or a healthy support system that can walk with you through the difficult times, join community groups, healthy online communication, or interaction with others who have been through or are going through a similar situation.

- Take the high road. This involves self-control and maturity. Think through your reaction and respond appropriately and in a timely way. Truth and strength in character always wins, but it is also seldom revealed at the onset of a situation. Stand in your truth, and in the end, truth and good character will prevail.

- Some people in your life are there to stay, but not everyone in your life gets to sit in the front row of your life — only people who support and value your hopes and dreams get to sit there. Think of it as an old movie theater with a balcony, where you get to move toxic people around in different seats far away from you, and they don't even know it.

- Be what you want to see in others. If you want a kind and gentle person, then you be kind and gentle. If you want an honest person, then you have to be honest. Remember that birds of a feather flock together. If you show me five of your closest friends, I can tell you who you are.

- Life begins at the edge of your comfort zone. If you are willing to make yourself uncomfortable enough to learn a new way of being, you are on the road to flourishing relationships, and to become a magnet for others to flourish. You don't have to embrace everything to which you are exposed, but keep an open mind, and you'll find that the more you get to know, the more you want to know.

- The serenity prayer can be a constant source of growth; it has been for me. In case you don't know, it reads, "God grant me the serenity to accept the things I cannot change, the courage to change the things I can, and the wisdom to know the difference."

Patricia Russell is a retired business executive specializing in results-oriented customer care and large-scale event planning. She is an ardent advocate for human rights and dignity for all people.

Onward!

By Jan White

Surprises. Cancer is certainly an unwelcome surprise. But there are good surprises hidden along the path. Magnificent surprises, in the form of new pathways you never imagined before.

We had been living the American dream. I married my college sweetheart, Michael. We have an awesome son, Ethan. Mike and I have run a successful small business, Meetings by Design, for more than 25 years.

I love being active and studied martial arts, achieving a third-degree black belt in kenpo karate after almost 15 years of study. But just one year later, in April 2016, our lives were forever changed when I was diagnosed with aggressive, Stage IV Non-Hodgkins Lymphoma that had invaded my chest and my spinal column.

I went from running the business with Mike, teaching kickboxing, and studying for my fourth-degree black belt to needing a walker.

I endured five-and-a-half months of intense chemotherapy that included 96 continuous hours of chemo every three weeks. I also received multiple injections to my ommaya, a head port implanted to get the chemo to my spine. Then we did a round of high-dose, high-risk in-patient chemo, followed by almost a month of radiation.

I was pronounced in remission.

I am here.

It wasn't until a year after I completed treatment, at a checkup with my oncologist, Dr. Shah, to whom I am quite certain I owe my life, that I learned just how close we had come. He told me that my file was dropped on his desk at 8:30 a.m. By 8:45 a.m., the partners had met about my situation. By 9:00 a.m., they called me to say, "Be in this office in one hour, pack a bag, you are not going home, you are being admitted to the hospital directly from the office. We have to begin chemo today. We have to try and save your spinal cord and your life." By 10:00 a.m., I was in Dr. Shah's office for our first appointment.

By noon, I was admitted to the hospital. I was cycled through heart study, lung study, blood work, a PICC line shoved in my arm, and by late afternoon, I was on chemo.

Our heads were spinning.

But the speed was crucial because the consensus was that I was seven to 10 days from being completely paralyzed and three weeks from dying. That of his career, I was his full-blown emergency.

But I'm here.

On our 30th wedding anniversary, a year and a half later, I was here to play with Michael in Disney World like two little kids, just like we did on our honeymoon.

Then, five years later, when Ethan married his beautiful bride, Marissa, I was here to dance — truly dance — with our son at their wedding.

I was here for a thousand moments of simple joy with family and friends.

But make no mistake, I am not a hero. I am not a saint. And I am not impervious to the naked terror that comes with what we now call "the Adventure."

That became clear to me during my third night in the hospital, when I sent this message to my best friend, Robbie, at 4:00 a.m. "I think the

numb is wearing off. Reality is setting in. Oh G-d, how did I get here? I'm unashamed to say I'm scared. Am I strong enough for this? I don't feel very strong right now. But I have too many people I love."

I wrote that as I lay alone in a hospital bed, at 4:00 a.m., wide awake, staring at my PICC line, listening to the air in line alarm go off, again, when the crushing enormity of my situation slammed into me.

Fear is something that everyone deals with in their own way. With cancer, there's a lot to face. At checkups, I am always asked to rate my anxiety, rate my depression, but I was stunned at how reluctant I was to say I was struggling.

As women, we are taught from an early age that you just handle it, all of it, no matter what. Be a good wife, mother, sister, aunt, friend, professional. I'll confess I needed some prodding to face the fear and the flood of other emotions.

My Aunt Eileen, who is truly the older sister I never had in all the best ways, called me a few months into the Adventure and asked if I was talking to anyone. I told her I was fine. She shot right back at me, "You are *not* fine. How could you possibly be fine? You are staring down Stage IV cancer in your spine. Go talk to someone, please."

And she was right. I did need to talk to someone, and I still talk to someone, as I continue to navigate the challenging reality of cancer and survivorship.

And I believe every member of my care team deals with fear and a flood of emotions as they care for me and their other patients. They're just exceptionally adept at hiding their emotions under their professional façades. But I did get to see a crack in that façade, once.

About a year after my treatment, Mike and I were producing a fundraiser for the one of the cancer centers where I was treated. Ironically, they were clients before the Adventure, and Dr. Shah was on the guest list.

I had a check-up a few weeks before the event, and I thanked him for planning to attend. He asked me how I knew, and I explained that we were producing the event.

Event night came and I went to thank him before he left. I asked if he enjoyed the event. He told me the event was lovely, but what he truly enjoyed was watching me run around the room, managing it. For the first time, I could see a crack in that professional façade in his very broad smile.

And I realized what he saw that day was me, not *cancer Jan*, but *me*. Me, managing a large black-tie event, being me. Yes, I had some help and modifications that didn't exist before, like assistants for when my legs gave out. Even now, there are days I turn to Mike for help when I need it. And pain management is essential every day, especially on event days.

But that day, even with modifications, for the very first time, he saw the real *me* and I could see the joy in his eyes. What a wonderful gift! For both of us.

Coming out of treatment, I knew I wanted to do something to give the Adventure purpose, but I had no idea how to accomplish this. Then I heard a radio interview with a member of Congress as he discussed repealing the Affordable Care Act, which was being debated in the U.S. House of Representatives. In the interview, he essentially said, "Why should good people have to pay for those with pre-existing conditions?" That got my attention.

Wasn't I a good person? Do people believe that those with pre-existing conditions deserved less treatment than others? Didn't we deserve to live, too? Apparently not, according to some people.

That was the day I decided to become an advocate. I registered as a Volunteer Legislative Patient Advocate with the American Cancer Society Cancer Action Network and the Leukemia & Lymphoma Society.

As an advocate, I meet with state and federal lawmakers on legislation that affects cancer patients and their families. I raise my voice to make a difference.

As an events producer, I was accustomed to working in the background. Stepping into the role of advocate was a new and uncomfortable place at first, but one that has become incredibly rewarding. The first time I felt empowered over this beast called cancer was when I first walked up the steps of Capitol Hill as an advocate.

I continued to raise my voice and was stunned when I was asked to speak professionally. While I had never envisioned this path for myself, I decided if I can help one person by speaking, then I should. This led to the creation of Jan Says Onward.

During the worst moments of the Adventure, my mantra was "Onward!" It is still Onward!

Jan Says Onward is my way of raising my voice to make a difference for cancer patients and their families by speaking to healthcare organizations, industry associations, cancer survivors, women's groups, or any organization facing a significant challenge. My presentations feature stark honesty, injected with humor, to motivate people to inspiration and action.

And I am grateful.

Onward!

Jan White is a successful small business owner, Stage IV cancer survivor/thriver, third-degree black belt in karate and professional speaker who combines stark honesty and wry humor for memorable presentations.

"Life is a Box of Chocolates"

By Jennifer D. Ryan

"My mama always said, 'Life is like a box of chocolates. You never know what you're gonna get.'" - Forest Gump

I grew up thinking that a career was all that I wanted. I could not wait to graduate from high school, attend the University of Wisconsin-Madison, and start my career. I never saw myself as being a stay-at-home mom or enjoying motherhood. Little did I realize what life had in store for me.

I grew up on a dairy farm in rural Wisconsin. Education was never an emphasis in our household. My father had an eighth-grade education and my mother got as far as 10th grade. Everyone in the family worked hard on the farm. We all had chores to do, ranging from milking and feeding the cows to growing our own food and managing the household of nine people.

Being a curious child, I was always reading and saw education as a gateway to leaving behind this rural life, which did not feel comfortable to me. After graduating near the top of my high school class and without financial or emotional support from my family, I moved to Madison to attend my dream school. After graduating with a bachelor's degree, I worked for several years. Because I wanted to change the world, I went on to get a law degree. The skills of hard work and perseverance learned as a child on the farm helped me during my many struggles to earn my degrees.

Finally, my career was starting to take shape. After a brief stint with an insurance company, I landed my dream job as an assistant attorney general for the Wisconsin Department of Justice. What more could I want? I was on top of the world.

Then, after two years practicing law, I found myself experiencing flu-like symptoms. Weeks went by with no improvement, and it became clear that I could not return to work full-time. Months went by with no diagnosis. I was devastated. My career seemed to be slipping away. I switched to working part-time but continued to have health issues and was diagnosed with a little-understood debilitating chronic condition.

Fortunately, once again, the resilience that I learned at an early age on the farm kept me going.

Several years later I married, and we bought a house together. I also realized I wanted children. I was in my late 30s and living with a chronic illness — not exactly a good candidate for motherhood. In fact, most people discouraged me from becoming a mom.

The road to motherhood was not easy. At age 40, I was considered high risk. My first pregnancy ended in a miscarriage, and I was devastated. During my second pregnancy, I was sick every day, and my doctors were concerned when I lost instead of gained weight. Because I was exhausted all the time, I had to quit my part-time work. I spent much of the last trimester in bed or on a recliner after I experienced pre-term labor in my sixth month. But finally, just before my due date, I delivered a beautiful, healthy baby girl.

Taking care of a baby while dealing with my chronic illness was not easy. However, I really wanted this baby and had gone through so much to have her. I thought I would miss my career after her birth. What I found, however, was much more precious. I found that motherhood was much more rewarding than practicing law had ever been.

Motherhood was a gift. Being a stay-at-home mom allowed me to follow my curiosity and desire for lifelong learning with my child. We decided to homeschool our daughter since both her parents are lifelong learners. Homeschooling helped us find a pace in our family life that accommodated my chronic illness and allowed our family to explore our interests and spend time together.

Today, I marvel at how my life has changed over the years and how distant I am from the dream I had as a teen. While I still feel a sense of loss for that dream, I found my success and happiness as a stay-at-home mom. I can sincerely say that every new chocolate from the box of life has enriched my journey.

Jennifer D. Ryan is a retired attorney and avid lifelong learner who supports women living their dreams.

Fitting In

By Pam Baker

It really is true that no matter where your path may take you, the roots begin in your childhood. I was raised in a very loving, lower-middle–income family with two parents and three siblings. We went to church on Sunday, ate every meal together, and were held to strict account.

Because my father was disabled at 30, my mother got a job outside the home, which was unusual at the time.

My dad made sure his children did well in school, worked as soon as they could, and made it to college. He pushed hard. If you brought home grades that were all A's, he wanted to know why they weren't A+'s. I took that to heart and applied myself to achieve what he dreamed for me. From my mother, I inherited a pure joy for life. Always the optimist, she had a life more difficult than she ever imagined, but she was happy and saw her glass as always half full. The combination of my mom and dad meant that I always worked hard, dreamed big, and approached at each new challenge with a positive outlook.

In school, I got good grades and had friends who also excelled. Their lives were very different from mine, coming from wealthier families with better homes, clothes, and food. I didn't feel that I really *fit in* because of my economic background. This even extended to academic achievements, like never really feeling like I belonged in the National Honor Society.

When I was 14, I started my first afterschool job. Although that meant no sports, band, or other school-based activities, I thrived at my McDonald's job. I loved the fast pace and excitement of the restaurant. McDonald's was a big deal in our community—the first fast food restaurant in town. The money I made and scholarships I earned helped get me to college. I was sure that when I got there, I would be like everyone else. I was sure I would fit in.

In college, however, the struggle actually became more real. I needed my work study job and another part-time job to keep up with expenses. But it was not enough if I wanted to go out with my dorm room friends and dress with the latest trends to fulfill my desire to fit in. At one point in my junior year when my major was the toughest, I had three part-time jobs.

Going home for the holidays, my grades arrived before me, and my father was waiting. I had gotten a C in intermediate accounting; accounting was my major. My father was livid and accused me of goofing off, not applying myself, and not trying hard enough. I was devastated. If I told him that I had three jobs just to fit in, he would tell me to quit one of them.

I knew I had to start standing up for what I wanted. I told my parents that I was working hard and was going to succeed but, if they continued to judge me so harshly, I would not come home again. That hit a nerve, and my father backed down and actually broke down. Even though he wanted us to have so much, he had pushed just a little too hard. Things changed for the better. Of course, that was also the only C I ever received, and I doubled down on making a strong finish.

I had finally arrived. I was a college graduate and now would fit in with the professionals. I bought two very expensive suits to start my first job as an auditor with the Commonwealth of Virginia. It was 1980, and I was the only female in my department. The men at the top were older. They didn't look or act like me. For most of them, their experience with women was a wife who was at home cooking and cleaning. They did not

194

know what to do with a 5-foot 3-inch female powerhouse of energy who was overly anxious to learn and wanted to get to the top.

Once again, I was an outsider, but I still had my positive attitude and work ethic. My big break came when we were required to implement a new, statewide accounting system. The more senior members of our team did not easily learn something brand-new, especially when it relied more heavily on technology. I decided I would study the new system and prove my value. I became the go-to person on my team to explain and teach everyone else what they needed to know. I felt empowered enough to look for another job because one thing I discovered was that even though my newly developed skills were appreciated, they were not enough to overcome the gender and age bias.

I joined a CPA firm in another state that provided tax and accounting services to local businesses. I was encouraged that there were two women owners at the firm and thought moving to a smaller community would help me overcome my belief that I did not belong because of my background. Once again, I dressed the part and showed up looking like a professional. Ironically, this time I didn't fit in because I looked so out of place compared to my peers, who were more rural and casual. I worked hard and learned a lot about taxes and small business. I also realized that I loved the world of audit. Both my first job and this one exposed me to audits of local governments and nonprofits.

My big lesson came when I was sent to a high-powered meeting with a real estate developer. I was representing one of my firm's small-business owners who had joint business dealings with the developer. The partner in my firm who was responsible for our client was out on maternity leave but assured me I could handle the meeting. She was wrong. The real estate developer spared no words in letting me know that I had failed. When I reported back to the partner, she told me to *shake it off* because it was normal to be treated like that as a woman. She told me that I should get used to it because the men would never accept that we were as smart as them. That was not the message that I wanted to hear and certainly not the life I wanted to live.

After much soul searching, I decided to follow my passion and work 100 percent in audit. I also wanted to be closer to where I grew up. I joined a CPA firm located outside Philadelphia that specialized in auditing governments and nonprofits. Finally, I was near a big city, serving the types of clients I enjoyed, and using my skills. I was also joining a firm with a very strict professional dress code. I loved it. I would finally fit in.

What was interesting is that I did fit in, but not for the reasons that I anticipated. Instead, I saw my young self over and over, as I worked with organizations that existed to support their communities. I could relate to programs that made a difference for someone who was from a low-income background. I could relate to a local government working to manage taxpayer funds to provide services to the community. I understood what it was like to budget tight to pay real estate taxes on a small home. I discovered I was really good at applying my technical skills to audit reports, but more importantly, I could meet with a board of directors or elected officials and make their audit and financials mean something. I could relate the results to what they were trying to achieve. They listened to me.

Although I was the only female in a management position when I joined my firm, I learned early on that when I produced results, I would be rewarded. That was deeply gratifying. I advanced to a full equity partner in my first two years and continued on that path to managing partner.

Yes, I worked harder and was driven to succeed. But the reason was that I had found my path and passion. My authentic self could thrive and grow because I could appreciate the journey and use it to propel me onward.

Pam Baker CPA CGFM, is an advocate for the accounting profession and serves as the Managing Partner of a regional progressive public accounting firm.

Who Am I?

By Cindy DelGiorno

I spent the first 47 years of my life not knowing who I was.

That's not entirely true. I spent the first 47 years of my life knowing only the half of it.

My story starts on September 1, 2020, when I was sitting at my makeshift desk, in my makeshift home office, across from my 5-year-old son. Our laptops were opened in front of us, with the backs of our screens touching. Both of us were struggling to pay attention to the screens. He was engaged in the Zoom version of kindergarten. I had just signed off on the daily morning Zoom with my coworkers. We were navigating the pandemic of 2020 together.

Scrolling through my email, I saw one from 23andMe. Months earlier, my friend Julia, after doing her own 23andMe test, had encouraged me to try this DNA thing. I initially dismissed the idea. My family was fairly boring, I thought. I was fairly boring. I didn't see any reason for paying $99 to confirm how boring my lineage was. I did have a spark of hope, though. I've always loved a good story.

Yet, since Covid-19 kept us all inside, working from home, my checking account had a little more ka-ching. I was spending on things I normally consider frivolous. When Julia mentioned the $99 DNA test again, I said,

"Why not? "and ordered the test. When the box from 23andMe arrived, it sat in my office for several weeks. One day, staring at the four walls of my office, I spotted it there. On a whim, I had ordered this test. On a whim, I opened the box and then followed the directions. I mailed off my sample to the lab, and promptly forgot about it. Then, about a month later, the email from 23andMe arrived.

Before I continue, let me give you a little bit of my backstory. My parents met at a dance, in the Bronx, where they both lived with their families. They married in 1965. I was born in 1972. A few years later, we moved to a three-family apartment house in Queens. It was truly a family home. My mom's sister lived on the top floor with her husband and two children. We lived on the second floor, and my grandparents lived on the first. We were close. I went up and down the stairs several times a day. I always felt safe and loved. My cousins were my best friends.

But it wasn't all sunshine. Everyone probably heard my parents arguing. My older sister was starting to get into trouble in school, out of school. She was often grounded. My parents divorced when I was 7 and my sister was 9. We were more relieved than upset.

Once my father moved out, he found an apartment across town. My mom would send us off, in a taxi, for weekend visits. Sometimes we begged not to go. My sister later said he was abusive. He could definitely yell, and he wasn't a fascinating conversationalist, but he had redeeming qualities. Sometimes he had a good sense of humor. I think I may have loved him because he adored me. His face lit up when I walked into a room. While my sister had her challenges growing up, I was easygoing and agreeable. While my sister seemed to cause him so much frustration and anger, I seemed to bring him joy.

My sister and I were not close. During the summer, I went to overnight camp. My sister was there, too, although it was hard to tell — she didn't acknowledge her dorky little sister. She quickly made friends and left me to fend for myself. My mother had two sisters, and they were all very close. I had one sister, and there were worlds between us. I was envious of friends who had good relationships with their siblings.

I often wished my mother would have more children. When I asked my mom why she did not, she replied that she wanted to, but not with my father. Apparently, the divorce had been coming for a long time. I secretly hoped to one day find out I had more siblings, and perhaps a wonderful sister who would become my best friend. I hoped that one day, we would discover that my father cheated on my mother and there would be another sister out there for me, completely different from the sister I had.

My father remarried. His new wife was from Tennessee and had a thick southern drawl. My sister and I flew to visit him one summer. I was surprised at how happy I was to see him. He worked the second shift, and she worked the day shift. That summer, I was 12, and spent most of my time alone, reading every book my stepmother had on her shelves. I read every single Danielle Steel book. My father liked to watch "All My Children" while we had lunch, before he went to work. When my stepmother came home from her office job, she made us all dinner, and we settled in for an evening of "Falcon Crest" and "Dynasty." I found myself fascinated by the soap opera storylines. Virtually anything was possible.

My 14-year-old sister spent her summer days exploring the neighborhood, making friends. Soon, my father was complaining that my sister was hanging out with "the gigaboos" in the neighborhood. He had several more insulting names. The man who grew up in the Bronx seemed to have lost any appreciation for diversity. I found myself liking him less. His new family called him a Yankee and seemed entertained by our NYC accents.

My mother remarried, and we moved to "the country," as my cousins said. My stepfather owned his own business and liked investing. My father called my stepfather "Moneybags." He had names for everyone, especially since he had moved to Tennessee. Most names were based on race, but some were based on other nonsensical things. The negativity seemed to take the oxygen out of the room. It made my sister and me very uncomfortable. We stopped visiting him in Tennessee. I enjoyed my life with my mom and stepfather.

Life went on. At age 34, I was about to be married and ready to have children; something I had dreamed about for as long as I could remember. Six weeks before my wedding, I found out I had breast cancer.

The oncologist told us that chemotherapy treatment would end my menstrual cycles. The chance of my fertility returning was 50/50. I was told that any eggs remaining would probably be damaged. I will never forget that day. Sitting in the sterile medical office with the oncologist and my fiancé, I contemplated a life without my own children. Gut-wrenching sobs tore through my chest. I cried until I was numb.

The oncologist suggested I harvest embryos, just to be on the safe side — even if my menstrual cycles did not return, I could still try for children. The fertility specialists could do amazing things, he assured us.

Before starting chemotherapy, my new husband and I did a round of IVF. We filled out all the forms, did all of the genetic testing. I asked my mother hundreds of questions about our ancestry. I even called my father to ask him about our relatives. I researched all things fertility-related and shared my findings with my mother. She and I have always been very close, and nothing was off-limits. We talked about everything. She told me that she went to see a fertility specialist when she was in her 20s and not getting pregnant.

We ended up with 19 frozen embryos, and hope for the future.

Two years after I finished chemotherapy, I was cleared to try for a pregnancy. I got in the best shape of my life. The first transfer was a success. My daughter was born three weeks early, but healthy and beautiful. We went back to the fertility specialists several more times. Almost every time, I got pregnant. Eight weeks. 10 weeks. All miscarriages. We ran out of embryos. Fertility specialists told us that our chances of another successful pregnancy were between zero and 1 percent.

Our daughter was almost three years old. I desperately wanted a sibling for her. I knew in my soul there would be another child.

My mother encouraged me to try everything. "You only need one golden egg," she said. I even found a picture of a golden egg in an Easter issue of a magazine and decided to develop a vision board around it. I took all kinds of supplements, got acupuncture, and ingested foul-tasting Chinese teas for fertility from the acupuncturist. I cut out coffee and alcohol. I did fertility-enhancing yoga and meditation.

I was 41 years old. The statistics were not encouraging, but I was ready to do anything to meet my second child. I even researched adoption, embryo adoption, and foster care. I prayed.

My son was born three weeks after I turned 42. He was perfect. I was filled with gratitude. When I first looked into his eyes, I felt the same thing I felt when I looked into my daughter's eyes. "There you are…," I thought. It was as if I had been searching for lifetimes and reuniting with my own soul. My mom, her sisters, and everyone on my mother's side of the family said he looked exactly like me. He was the boy version of me. Same big brown eyes. Same face shape. Same expressions. Just as with my daughter, I was immediately smitten. Our family was complete.

Now, five years after his birth, I was clicking on that email from 23andMe. No initial surprises: My family DNA was all Eastern Europe and Russia. I was 99.8% Jewish. But then, I clicked on "View All DNA relatives" and saw five names at the top of the list, each called "half-sibling."

My first thought was that these online DNA tests were faulty. It probably meant cousins. With each of these people, it appeared that I shared at least 22% of my DNA. One name showed more than 32% shared DNA. So weird, I thought. What a waste of $99.

Still, I was intrigued enough to click on Connect with one of the names. He told me to message another name on the list. I sent her a message. She immediately responded and asked if I could take a call. Feeling like I was about to enter "The Twilight Zone," I said yes.

"Hi, Cindy," she said.

"So ... this is weird, right? It says you are my half-sibling. It must mean cousins ...," I started.

"Well ...Are your parents still alive?"

"Yes, both of them."

"Can you call your mom, and ask her about this?"

"I mean, it's not a sibling connection, right? I must have done the test wrong."

"You should call your mom, and then call me back. Will you do that?"

"We're not siblings, are we? The test is wrong, isn't it?"

By now, my son had left the room, probably to hide out in his bedroom upstairs, playing games on his iPad. Normally, I would redirect him back to class, but it felt like the world had stopped. I felt the heaviness of the moment. I was glad to be sitting at my desk, alone in my office.

"I really think you should call your mom. After that, I'll tell you everything."

"So, we *are* siblings? Do you mean my father had an affair?"

"Call her, OK? And then call me back."

"OK, I'll call her. Talk soon."

I Face-Timed my mother immediately. She and my stepfather were playing Mexican Train, and I saw all the tiles on their kitchen table. It seemed surreal, like I was on the brink of something terrifying and exciting at the same time. When I told her about the DNA test results, my stepfather's eyebrows went up. I knew immediately that he already knew the reason. It suddenly dawned on me that they both knew something I did not.

I asked my mom why these people came up as half-siblings.

She exhaled slowly and then told me her story.

She explained that after four years of marriage, she wasn't getting pregnant. She had always dreamed of being a mother. My mom was a retired kindergarten teacher who absolutely adored children. She went to a fertility specialist recommended by her OB/GYN. After testing, it was revealed that her husband was highly unlikely to father any children. As a couple, they agreed to use a donor and keep it a secret.

This was how it was done back then. They told no one.

After giving birth to my sister, my mother was referred to a different fertility specialist, on Park Avenue; the doctor she worked with previously was no longer taking fertility patients. They were told that the donor sperm would be mixed with her husband's sperm. It would be impossible to know, conclusively, who the father was. The donor — a medical student looking to make some extra money — would be similar in appearance to her husband.

The fertility doctor was there, in the hospital, to deliver me into the world. My mom remembered hearing him say, "You have a beautiful baby girl!" She smiled when she recalled this, and then continued. She admitted she didn't think about who the father might be. There was no way of finding out, and no reason to do so. I looked so much like my mother; no one suspected that I didn't belong to my parents.

The sister I grew up with had actually been my half-sister. The one sibling who called the same two people parents, was as much related to me as these five siblings.

My sister spent almost two years of her adolescence in a state school and hospital. Often she would refuse to see us when we went there for visits. She attempted suicide several times. Her diagnoses included borderline personality disorder, chronic depression, and eating disorders. During my pregnancies, I worried that my children would inherit her mental illnesses. She is the reason I studied counseling psychology and why I now work in the field. Several years ago, she succeeded in taking her own life. I was heartbroken that she would never know that our father was really no relation to us at all. I know she would have been relieved, too.

I called my "new" sister back, and she filled me in. At least 22 of us now show up on DNA sites.

Who was our biological father?

There were no donors.

Our father was the fertility doctor.

I felt lighter than I had in years. I was no relation to the man who insulted Obama and called Black people "gigaboos" or "Southern Canadians." I had siblings! I wanted to meet them all. Every one of us came from a mother who desperately wanted to know US. There is something beautiful and powerful about that. A few days later, we all participated in a Zoom. I felt at home. I knew these people. It was as if we had always known each other, and were now reunited. Many months later, when some of us got together for lunch, it was like a new world opened up. This world was comfortable and known, although it couldn't possibly be.

I was 47 years old when I made a shocking discovery about my true identity. I could be angry at my mother, or at my stepfather who knew the whole time, or at the doctor who brazenly ignored ethics in reproductive medicine. I'm more surprised than anything. And I'm grateful to be alive. It's like a huge sunroof just opened as I drive through life. I feel like I've just unloaded a lot of baggage weighing me down. The sun is shining, and the wind is in my hair. Life is beautiful.

Cindy DelGiorno runs the Life Skills program at a women's prison. She also does sales and marketing for an e-commerce wine business.

Bridging the Gap
in Cancer Care

By Sue Weldon

When my doctor told me I had breast cancer at the age of 39, my first thought was of my three young children. I wanted to be there to raise them, to see them grow up, and to be strong for them.

I had been running myself ragged that year, racing between commitments with my children, coaching gymnastics, and taking care of my mom, who had a difficult cancer diagnosis. The day would begin with a quick cup of coffee to get me going and, before I knew it, the day was over, often without my having eaten anything of substance. I was on the go, caring for all, and not recognizing my own needs. My mom died in February that year, and in April, I was diagnosed with cancer when my doctor found a sizable lump in my breast that had gone undetected.

I underwent an arduous treatment regime of a bilateral mastectomy and six months of chemotherapy. I struggled with debilitating side effects — night sweats, hot flashes, headaches, bone pain, anxiety, weight loss, and nausea.

After surgery and chemotherapy treatments were complete, I was told that I was cancer-free. Despite this wonderful news, I hardly recognized the depleted woman I saw in the mirror. I was determined to regain some control of my health. With a great deal of prayer, I dove into educating myself and finding resources to address my needs. I discovered a lot of research showing that integrating complementary therapy could significantly improve patient well-being during cancer treatment and beyond. I reached out to friends, colleagues, and contacts in the health field, and began incorporating acupuncture, massage, yoga, exercise, and nutrition into my recovery plan. I experienced significant reduction in pain, increased energy, and improvement in overall wellness.

It was life changing.

Fast-forward a year and I was feeling like my old self again, restored, and in a better place. I was able to get back to some of my old routine, with a new lens — and a new understanding of my own self-care.

On my way to a yoga event in Philadelphia one Sunday morning, I noticed a young woman across the art museum steps. She had a balding head, hollow eyes, and yellow skin. I was looking in a mirror and saw myself in her. I walked over to her, ready to share all the tools I had learned about, to empower her as well. I remember saying to her, "I was where you are today, just one year ago. It will be a tough hard year, but you will get through it. You will get to the other side." The young woman looked at me and said, "You look so good. What did you do?" I told her I called on a friend to walk me through private sessions of yoga on my deck, and had 36 treatments of acupuncture, and I dove into food as my medicine, switching to a plant-based diet." And the woman began to tear up. "Good for you," she said, "But I could never afford all that."

Ahh, there was the gap. I was able to take the much-needed time to heal and had the financial access to the complementary therapies. I realized that very few breast cancer patients in active treatment or recovery have the time and energy to do the research about, and the financial means to commit to, the treatments. I was ashamed for missing that gap.

At that moment, Unite for HER was born.

Fueled by the powerful impact that complementary therapies had on me, I founded Unite for HER to bridge the gap between the medical and wellness communities and bring integrative complementary therapies to all breast and ovarian cancer patients, regardless of income.

Since 2009, Unite for HER has served more than 15,800 breast and ovarian cancer patients across the nation by partnering with more than 60 hospitals and nonprofit organizations in all 50 states.

Our dynamic, creative, innovative team leads with purpose to get our wellness program to all those who need it. We have much work that lies ahead, but the path is very clear.

There is a quote I love, and I say it often because it rings so true for what we have seen over the years:

"If you pour a lot of love and support into someone or something, it is bound to flourish."

That is our Unite for HER. We are at an exciting time and together, we are changing the lives of thousands of people across the nation.

Sue Weldon is the Founder and CEO of Unite for HER, a national nonprofit for those affected by breast and ovarian cancer.

Becoming a Leader for Change

By Mengdi (Mandy) Tao

Growing up in the largest agricultural province in China, I had limited understanding of the world outside my small town. My parents were busy with their business, so my grandparents played a significant role in my upbringing. My grandmother had traditional views about gender roles and did not see the value in educating girls. However, my grandfather had a more progressive outlook and encouraged me to pursue my education and explore the world beyond our town. His support became the foundation of my journey toward becoming a leader for change.

During my time in university, I join the World Academy for the Future of Women program. I found myself in a diverse environment where I was exposed to new ideas and perspectives. It was during my time here that I discovered my passion for making a positive impact on the world. This program gave me the tools and knowledge I needed to start my journey. It instilled a strong foundation for my future development.

After completing my studies, I embarked on a career that allowed me to make a difference: I became the program director for one of China's most influential family foundations, where I worked to improve educational opportunities for underprivileged children in rural areas. Through art programs, sex education, and other initiatives, we aimed to make a difference in the lives of these children.

I also oversaw more than 15 programs focused on promoting family philanthropy. I organized one of the first family philanthropy forums in China, which sought to promote the concept of giving back to society. This was a groundbreaking event that inspired many people to start their own philanthropic initiatives.

Throughout my career, I have remained committed to supporting women. I have taken on various roles in different organizations, such as the Women Empowerment Council, where I organized the Women's Empowerment Forum and Awards in China. This event has become one of the largest gatherings of women leaders in business and has had a significant impact on empowering women in the workplace.

My commitment to women's empowerment was tested early in my career when I was offered a job at a company where the boss showed no respect for his female employees. I refused the offer and explained that I did not want to work for a company that did not respect its female employees. This experience reinforced my belief in the power of being a strong woman and supporting other women in achieving their goals.

Recently, I founded Global Youth Action, an organization aimed at inspiring and empowering young people across the world to become active global citizens and leaders. Our goal is to create a network of future leaders and support them in making transformational change.

My journey has not been without its challenges.

Growing up in a traditional family with a culture of gender inequality was not easy, but with the support and encouragement of my grandfather, I was able to break free from those limitations. Similarly, working in a male-dominated industry and advocating for female empowerment has come with its own set of challenges, but I have remained committed to my mission of creating positive change in the world.

As I reflect on my journey, I am grateful for the opportunities I have had and the people who have supported me along the way. My experiences have taught me valuable lessons about the importance of education, perseverance, and the power of a supportive community. Looking ahead, I am excited to continue my work in creating positive change and inspiring the next generation of leaders to do the same.

Mengdi (Mandy) Tao is a passionate advocate for women and youth, an experienced philanthropy advisor, and a dedicated global community builder. She is committed to driving positive social impact across the globe.

What Was Missing?

By Melissa K. Gonville

Have you ever felt like something was missing in your life and you just couldn't put your finger on it? Feeling a little lost, a little down, but also thinking that it didn't make sense to feel that way, given all your blessings?

That was me in late 2007. I was in my late 30s and successful in so many aspects of my life. I was a managing director at a major financial institution; happily married to my high school sweetheart, Greg; had two healthy children who were the loves of my life along with my husband. We had a nice house and many friends and family with whom we could spend time and enjoy life. I was known for being that person who was always smiling, an eternal optimist. I could always find the best in people.

So why was I feeling this gap, this missing piece in my heart and my life?

I had many discussions with my husband, my boss, and my friends to try to figure out what I needed to change. Not knowing what else to do, I put my feelings aside and moved forward with my life. Then an amazing thing happened (and I almost missed it): I found my purpose.

I was leading the women's networking group at Chase in Delaware at the time, and we wanted to partner with an organization that aligned with our mission of empowering women. We reached out to YWCA Delaware and partnered with them by serving on committees, volunteering, and leading events. I personally volunteered to lead the auction for their annual Evening of Style event. After months of hard (fun) work, we hosted a successful event with live and silent auctions. The YWCA CEO asked me to join the board of directors, where I could make a bigger impact with a longer-term commitment to the organization. I agreed.

One day, about a year later, I had the realization that the feeling of missing something in my life — that gap — was long gone. I was so busy focusing on my life, my work, and my board service that I hadn't even realized it was gone. I had found my purpose — empowering women — and I was doing it in very real, tangible ways.

After a year on the board of directors, I was asked to take on the role of president-elect, a precursor to becoming president of the board. I had a new job that was all-consuming and hesitated to take on more responsibility. I talked to Greg and his response was, "Do you want to do it? Will it make you happy? Then we will make it work — we always do." I took on the role and, of course, we made it work. It was a fantastic experience.

I've mentored many people over the course of my career, and I have often offered this advice: If something is important to you and will help you fulfill your purpose, then you will make it work. And it will probably be among the most rewarding things you've ever done.

Fast-forward to this past year, when I left my corporate job in pursuit of something new and different. It was scary, but I also felt rejuvenated by the many possibilities. Within three months, I received an offer to be the interim CEO of YWCA Delaware, the organization that has had my heart for 15 years. Six months later, I became the official CEO. It has always been my dream to find a job that aligns with my purpose, passion, and values, and where I can feel fulfilled daily by doing good in the world.

The stars aligned, and so the next chapter of my story begins.

Melissa Gonville is a Business Executive who, after 31 years in Corporate roles, followed her passion for people and for diversity, equity and inclusion into the non-profit sector.

Teaching Myself How to See in the Dark

By Mary Schreiber Swenson

My story begins in a small rural town of 700 people in Eden Valley, Minnesota. My father was the local dentist and my mother a housewife. We would pack up our lunches and walk to school every day, go to church every Sunday, and never really venture out of our farming community.

I did what I do best and set up lemonade stands on every corner and created a babysitting notebook in which all the girls would come through me to get assignments. I think this was my very first franchise.

We never had any mentors. I knew I was different, and the more I tried to conform, the stronger the fire became in my belly. I knew that I had a vision far beyond the cornfields, but had no idea there was any other life. Our high school never taught us geography—my social studies teacher informed me that I would never leave the state and home economics would serve me much better than a map.

Then one day, while I was running my lemonade stand on the only main street that ran through our small town, a large black Cadillac passed through with the most beautiful woman I had ever seen. She was wearing a white, collared shirt with a fur around her neck. She had a long, slender cigarette holder and puffed her cigarette slowly. Her hair was in a blonde bob with loose locks of curls around her face. For some reason, she made a huge impact on my life, maybe because we were not allowed to watch TV and she seemed to me the closest to a movie star that I had ever seen. She was also alone in the car—free to drive, free to be whatever she desired—and for just that moment, I also felt free.

I could not believe my eyes, and from that day forward, I did not know what I was going to do with my life, but I knew what freedom looked like.

I went on to college, career, and motherhood. Then my mother died at the age of 54 of an operable brain aneurysm, so I returned to my small hometown and decided to bring my two younger brothers to my new home in Delaware. At this point, I had three small children and two brothers I was caring for; I worked full-time and went to school full-time, eventually getting my PhD in economics from Walden University.

My journey was not an easy one, and I found myself so angry at the healthcare system: Because my mother lived in a rural area and did not have access to quality healthcare, she died too young. So, I set out on a journey to change the healthcare system. I was not going to rest until I made an impact on how people received healthcare.

Committed to creating powerful change, I become an innovator and distributor who has started a revolution to change the face of dental and healthcare globally. I launched several companies, including MyMedChoices and MySmileChoices, a global dental, medical, and wellness second-opinion organization. I am driven by the mission to help women achieve economic empowerment and success.

By connecting to my core, I am creating a life that I adore. To be successful, I had to teach myself how to see in the dark.

Mary Schreiber Swenson, PhD, Founder CEO, MyMedChoices & Guava Healthcare, a public company; Harvard Women's Leadership Board Member; published author; Lifetime Achievement Award recipient; 100 Women to KNOW recipient.

From Bullied to Brave

By Ruth E. Thaler-Carter

Until writing this essay, I was never very introspective; I act on instinct and am pleasantly surprised when things turn out right. This has been empowering.

Today, I may be the poster child for extroverts, and no one who knows me now will believe that I was shy and reserved as a child.

It didn't help that when I was 9, my family moved to a new neighborhood and school system — in December, smack-dab in the middle of the school year. The good thing: A lifelong friend lived right down the block, and I had met some of her friends in the neighborhood. The bad: We were in different classrooms, and her family moved to Philadelphia in the new year.

Most of my new classmates had known each other since nursery school, and already had friends and cliques. It didn't help that after only half a year, we joined kids from several elementary schools in one junior high. Many of us felt lost and at sea, although there were lots of new people to connect with. But for me, it was two major upheavals in only a few months.

Junior high was very hard. I was mocked for things I couldn't change or control: curly hair, liking to read, being one of the first to not just wear but need a bra, and more. I focused my pain on the meanest guy rather than every mean kid, which helped me keep my sense of self: I'm not a hater. My parents were supportive when I let them know what was going on, but I rarely did that.

I learned some important elements of personal power by figuring out what was really me and what was worth adjusting to appease peer pressure. And when a popular teacher attempted to molest me, somehow I knew to get away from him before anything could go farther than a closed classroom door, drawn window shade, and flabby hand on my knee.

High school brought another influx of kids from other schools and a huge letdown: Our junior high school guidance counselor had promised that high school would be a whole new world, free from being mocked, and it was so not true. The mocking continued and spread to the new kids. It took about a year and a half to find a group of my own. It wasn't perfect, because I didn't do the drugs everyone else was enjoying, but it was a community of my own. Those friendships remain close to this day. And having that community went a long way to releasing the extrovert that's the real me.

In a way that I've come to recognize as a characteristic moment of power, I applied to be on the staff of my high school literary magazine and wasn't accepted — an especially bitter blow because everyone on the staff was a friend and even my brother was accepted — but I responded by starting my own literary magazine (I even let my brother participate). And convinced a local newspaper to let me write a column — that they paid for! — about happenings at school. Those were my first experiences in publishing and journalism, and they defined my path ever since, even if I didn't recognize that aspect at the time.

I felt out of it in another way: no boyfriends. Then I met my first love in the summer between junior and senior high school, at a program outside New York City. He happened to be Black. That took a little courage, because some of the other Black participants were into the Black Power movement and disapproved of interracial relationships. (Other aspects of that life-changing relationship are a story for another day.)

Over those years, some kind of personal strength was building up, and it came to the fore in 1974. A friend of someone I was dating knocked on my apartment door and asked if he could use my phone because his car had died. I let him in, and he attacked and raped me, threatening to kill me if I said anything. For some possible crazy reason, I called the police anyhow, filed a complaint, and took him to court, more because someone in the police department told me he had a history of child abuse incidents that had never been tried than on my own behalf. It went to trial twice, with a hung jury both times, and I gave up — but at least I tried to get him off the street. (And I was able to have good relationships with men afterward, which doesn't always happen to women who are violated.)

A few months later, he was arrested, charged, and eventually tried for the abduction, assault, and rape of two little girls and the murder of one of them. I was furious at the jurors who set him free to do such horrible things by letting him off in my case, but also felt a sense of pride that I had at least tried to do something about him.

In 1980, one of those "I quit/You're fired" situations coincided with the end of a relationship and I left St. Louis for a job in DC with an international magazine.

I took my professional life into my own hands in 1984 and launched a freelance writing, editing, and proofreading business (which, among good things, led to participating in this book project). It is a truly powerful and empowering feeling to put your career in your own hands.

These defining moments came in handy in 2005, when I chaired the first conference in years of a professional association I belonged to. To my surprise and annoyance, the board decided not to do another conference the following year. I was so annoyed that ... I created my own conference! I've organized and hosted it ever since, for the first year or so with a colleague and in the past two years in partnership with another association. It's been a wonderful, empowering experience that makes me glad that silly board wimped out back then.

Most recently, I found an unexpected level of personal power after my beloved husband, whom friends and colleagues knew as "Wayne-the-Wonderful," died after 30 great years together. We met in his native Baltimore and moved to my hometown of Rochester, New York, when he retired — I was willing to go back home because I figured my mom would need me sooner rather than later, and I can do my work anywhere.

Loss is different for everyone; some people stay where they were happy with a partner, but that didn't work for me. I kept expecting him to be there when I woke up or came back from errands, or at the grocery store (he loved going to Wegmans!), and I couldn't handle it. This emotional turmoil, along with an accident that left me unable to drive for three months and a new landlord, made me realize that it was time for a move. I needed a walkable neighborhood and a place with no connections to Wayne, even though he'll always be part of my heart.

A trip back to St. Louis, where I lived many years ago, proved that friendships and professional connections there were still in good shape. Everyone said things like, "What took you so long!"

Before I started to look at rental places as I had planned, I had an amazing opportunity to do something totally new: Buy a place to live. At 65! By myself! Without ever having a mortgage before! Everything seemed to line up as signs this was meant to be, and now I'm back in the Gateway City, owner of a beautiful condo and reconnected to old friends and colleagues while meeting new ones.

Friends have been telling me that I'm brave and strong, and that making such a big change after such a big loss was impressive and amazing. That feels very good but continues to surprise me. Very little of that process felt deliberate; it all just seemed to happen without much effort. It often feels like being admired for something I don't really deserve credit for.

I've been fired from a job, betrayed emotionally and physically attacked, rejected personally and professionally. I've lost the world's best parents and the world's most wonderful husband. But many of the contributors to this book have experienced even worse and reading their stories has filled me with admiration for our collective strength, resilience, and spirit of service. It's both humbling and inspiring to be part of it.

What all this comes down to is that bad things can have positive effects and figuring out who and what we are is vital to finding our power and creating lives worth living. Mine is a life I've made for myself, and that feels "Great"!

Ruth E. Thaler-Carter is a widely published, award-winning freelance writer, editor, proofreader, and speaker who is known as the Queen of Networking.

Stretching with Confidence

By Carol Parkinson Arnold

My life has been filled with moments of stretching in ways that built and reinforced my confidence. I was never told I couldn't do something because I was a girl. For example, before getting a driver's permit, I was required to change the oil and tires, as well as know the major parts of an automobile engine. And before being allowed access to the family car, I was required to learn to drive my father's truck with its three-on-the-tree manual transmission mounted on the steering column.

Travel has been a big way of stretching myself. When I was barely 17 years old, I did an 824-mile road trip from Keeseville, New York, to Nova Scotia with my two sisters and cousin. No reservations. Overnight in Bar Harbor, Maine. An eight-hour ferry trip to Halifax. A tent, sleeping bags, and some snacks. What were my parents thinking?

The next year, I asked my father if I should buy a stock car for the summer or go to Europe. He did not even blink before he responded: "Go to Europe!" I had never been on a plane, there was a phone strike going on, and I missed connecting with my travel group. But I made my way to Paris, celebrated my 18th birthday, and found my group. Then I went on to London and Amsterdam, and came back home with a new boyfriend.

On my first business trip, my mother asked who was going with me. I explained that the company didn't pay for me to have a travel companion. Since then, I've traveled across the U.S., Canada, and Europe on business, usually alone. My confidence also enabled me to totally change travel plans if I was stretching in a way that felt too dangerous. For example, a friend invited me to go skiing in New Zealand. I remember being in the Philadelphia airport in July with my ski bag, looking so smug. When I arrived in New Zealand, the roads to the ski resorts were very unsafe, with no guardrails and steep drop-offs. We left and went to Los Angeles instead. I had to go to Rodeo Drive for some summer clothes because our suitcases were packed for cold weather. My friend treated.

Stretching has also enabled me to get through some difficult times. In 1973, I married a man from Delaware in a candlelit double-wedding ceremony with my sister. Two years later, he was diagnosed with stage 4b Hodgkin's Disease. I had no idea where the hospital was and didn't know how to talk to doctors. I stretched and became confident as a caregiver during the eight remaining years of his life. In fact, I was the first person in Delaware to take someone home with an IV.

During that period, I was chosen to be a 1980 Olympic Torch Bearer, representing Delaware. One of 52 people on the Torch Team, I was selected based on running capability, poise, confidence, and my essay about how I embodied "the spirit of the whole man." My involvement included media interviews; public appearances; television shows like "Good Morning America" and "ABC Sports"; and meeting the Delaware governor, other public figures, and many Olympians. I gained even more confidence from this honor.

I have also brought confidence into one of my interests: real estate investment. I usually purchase real estate within 30 minutes of viewing, after doing my research and due diligence so I can be confident that I have the information necessary to make the right decision. To date, I have almost always at least tripled my investment when I've sold a property.

Today, I'm the happiest I have ever been. I'm back in my beloved North

Country New York mountains. One of my favorite things to do is drive my antique sports car with standard transmission. I'm near my mother, several siblings, and my youngest niece and nephew. I live in a beautiful place and am so fortunate.

I do have three pieces of advice for you. First, always keep your passport up to date so you can jet off to Paris for dinner. Two, when you have the opportunity to encourage young people to follow their dreams, please do so. And finally, *stretch!*

Carol Parkinson Arnold retired from DuPont Engineering as Knowledge Management Leader after almost 40 years. She now volunteers with Rotary, Clinton County Historical Association, Clinton Community College Alumni Board, Joint Council for Economic Opportunity, her HOA Board, and Great Dames.

The P.O.W.E.R. of
a Superwoman

By Nicolle D. Surratte

Power. Everyone has some degree of power. Power can manifest as strength, authority or influence. It can be demonstrated in actions or experienced through words. When I think about my life journey, I pause at the power of a word that forever changed my life: Cancer.

This is the word I heard over the phone in 2011 as I was leaving my office for the day. I can't recall anything the doctor said after this word. Every part of my being instantly went numb—my hand as I hung up the phone, my body as I moved in what felt like slow motion, my mind as I tried to process what a breast cancer diagnosis would mean.

The 13-mile drive home felt like an eternity. I stopped at a red light and noticed that the woman behind me was slightly overweight and smoking a cigarette. *Now, wait a minute*, I thought. *I never smoked and never drank. I carefully monitored what I ate and exercised regularly. Cancer?* No matter how the math teacher in me calculated, the equation didn't add up and the tears came streaming down.

I don't know how I made it home safely that afternoon, but when I pulled into the driveway, I knew that the woman who would enter was not the same woman who left that morning. As I walked through the door, the silence was so loud. Cancer.

My first call was to my "second mom." My biological mom was in a nursing home battling Alzheimer's. Mom #2 knew a lot about almost everything, especially health. I was confident she would steer me in the right direction.

She ruled out the local hospital near my hometown in Pennsylvania and instructed me to contact the Cancer Treatment Centers of America (CTCA) in Philadelphia.

With a strategy in place to secure a medical team, I knew these experts were only part of the picture. As a woman of faith, I would need God in ways I had not experienced before. The next call was to my spiritual mom. I not only needed and wanted her Godly wisdom and guidance; I needed her prayers.

I sat at the dining room table, trying to come to grips with how my life was about to change. The waterfall of tears didn't stop until God got my attention by taking me back 10 years when the "wuz-band" left. God reminded me that during the years I spent on "Separated Street" and "Divorce Drive," He supplied everything my children and I needed. Remembering how God did all of that and more, I knew He could and would handle a breast cancer diagnosis. My goal became living, by any means necessary.

After I called CTCA the next morning, things began to move at a rapid pace. There are five stages of breast cancer, 0 through 4, and I was diagnosed at Stage 0-1. I was an ideal candidate for Intraoperative Radiation Therapy (IORT). This procedure involves removing the tumor and administering radiation on the table. That's it. There would be no additional radiation treatments and no chemotherapy. *Yes!* I shouted on the inside. *This is great, 'cause I ain't got time for cancer. I've got things to do, places to go and people to see.*

IORT was supposed to be a simple procedure. The operative words are "supposed to be." After the surgery, I learned that the cancer had spread beyond what the initial tests revealed. I went from a Stage 0-1 to a Stage 3C, an aggressive cancer requiring aggressive treatment. The chemotherapy I hoped to avoid would now be my treatment starting point. Quickly, I reminded myself of the goal: living, by any means necessary.

That first chemo treatment was expected to last six-plus hours. As I waited to be assigned a chair and receive my chemo "cocktail," I received a call from the nursing home where my mom resided. As her caregiver, my permission was needed for hospice services to begin.

Three weeks later, the nursing home called again to inform me of her passing. It was hard to believe that the visit I had with Mom four hours earlier was our last. How was I to manage this? I was a single mom of two children in college. My family lived hours away in the Washington, DC, area. I was working full-time and getting chemo each week — chemo that left me too weak to clean the house, run the vacuum, or prepare meals. And now, I had a funeral to plan.

In the months that followed, chemo issues mounted as I struggled with low white blood cell counts. Treatment was delayed a week to give my body time to rebound. Unfortunately, that one week morphed into additional weeks and chemo was eventually discontinued. Plan B was now on the table: surgery #2. This surgery was successful, and I was able to finish the remaining chemo treatments and begin radiation. Treatment that should have been completed in six months took 18 months.

This cancer journey provided me with time to be still and reflect. Based on how I had taken care of myself since high school, the diagnosis was a surprise. From divorce, to diagnosis, to the death of my mom, I *thought* I was taking care of myself and managing my stress. However, I came to the conclusion that I was just really *busy*.

Women *are* busy — busy taking care of everyone and everything, often at the expense of their own health. I believe we are modern-day "Superwomen," dealing with a modern-day kryptonite called stress.

However, we can combat stress with self-care. And contrary to popular belief, self-care isn't selfish, but essential to every aspect of health: the physical, mental, emotional, spiritual, financial, occupational, and relational. As a holistic health coach for women and breast cancer "thriver," a diagnosis of any type should not be the wake-up call that forces women to pay more attention to their health and wellness practices.

The real power of a Superwoman goes beyond anything ever created in comic books or viewed on the big screen. It's only after we take care of ourselves that we can best take care of our personal and professional responsibilities. Here are a few ways Superwomen can tap into their **P.O.W.E.R.:**

P — Physical activity

Throughout the day, find ways to move more and sit less. Engaging in movement exercises that you enjoy increases the likelihood that you'll continue doing them. The options are many and range from Zumba, cycling, and swimming to yoga, walking, and gardening. (Be sure to consult your physician before starting anything new.)

O — Own your self-care

Put yourself on your "to do" list. If you don't, who will? Don't think of this as another chore. Instead, focus on activities that bring you joy. Make self-care a daily practice. Simply start with 5 minutes. Your self-care preferences may change over time, so give yourself grace and space.

W — Watch your appetite

Food is the fuel we need to function. Focus on eating to live, instead of living to eat. And eat as if your life depends on it, because it truly does. Increase your consumption of fruits and vegetables, and decrease your intake of fat, salt, and sugar. Avoid sugary beverages and reach for water.

E — Eliminate stress

The human body is wired to respond automatically to stressors. However, it's the long-term, chronic stress that can lead to chronic health conditions. Although we can't control people and/or situations, we can control our own responses. Identify your stress triggers as well as the stress management strategies that work best for you.

R — Rest

Rest is not just for babies and very young people. Restful and restorative sleep is equally important for adults. This is the time our bodies and minds need to reset and recharge. Create a sleep routine that includes powering down electronics and sleeping in a room that's cool, dark, and device-free.

And in case you're wondering, practicing self-care does *not* mean forfeiting your Superwoman status. You are a *Super Woman!* Don't *find* time for your health; *make* time. The decisions you make, or fail to make, move you closer to wellness, or closer to illness. Let self-care be your new superPOWER!

Nicolle D. Surratte, an inspirational speaker, breast cancer advocate and certified holistic health coach with A Health Coach for Me, helps women decrease stress, increase self-care and embrace lifestyle changes.

The Gift

By Maria Bynum

When my mother had Alzheimer's, I brought her home to live with me. This awful disease had robbed her of her words, personality, and ability to feed and bathe herself. In this reversal of roles, I found myself happy to have the honor of taking care of her, yet overwhelmed.

That's when I learned the value of having a village. A dear friend, who was an expert at caring for the elderly and disabled, helped me get the hospital bed and all the accessories necessary to address my mother's many needs. We arranged her room with bright-yellow accessories and placed her bed near the windows, where the morning sun would light up the entire room. It was cheerful and homey, with her favorite rocking chair near the bed.

My daughters and husband had a front-row seat to the switch in roles between my mother and me. They became daily participants and witnesses to what you do for someone you love when they can't do for themselves. Together we learned about home healthcare, caretakers, and that hospice doesn't have to be for those dying — it can be compassionate care for the living as well.

When my mother was in her right mind, she was a talker who did not mince her words. She could be direct with her comments, assertive,

241

and a commanding presence at family gatherings. She was a shopaholic and fashionista. This woman who lived in our home was so different. She was quiet, sweet, and docile. I missed her laughter, her life-of-the-party personality, and her take-charge attitude.

A registered nurse with two master's degrees and an impressive résumé, my mother dropped out of the workforce to care for her three children until we were in junior high school, before returning to her career for another 20 years. While working and caring for her family, she brought her father to our home to take care of him when he could no longer live on his own. I often marveled at how she managed work, kids, and caring for my grandfather.

Now life had come full circle: I too worked, managed my family, and brought my mother to live with me. I was doing what I had seen her do and learned the secret of her success those many years ago. It's a mother's love that helps her nurture her own children while providing tender loving care to a parent. I hope my children will mirror this rite of passage if or when I need help.

Life was chaotic as we all struggled with demanding schedules. Caregivers came in and out during the week to take care of my mother while we worked or went to school. They would sit and talk with my mother, read the newspaper and magazines to her, and play music because she always liked to dance. In the evenings and during the weekends, our family members were her sole caregivers.

I remember my husband sitting with my mom, teasing her, feeding her what he was eating, watching TV, and caring for her in a million different ways. My daughters would put lotion on her skin, comb and brush her hair, and help me put her to bed at night. My sister would spell us on the weekends by coming for the day and sitting with our mother so we could run errands, catch a movie, or go out for dinner. It was a labor of love on the part of my entire family and our friends and relatives.

On the rare occasions when my mother did speak, we felt inexpressible joy in hearing her express herself. One evening, my youngest daughter was adjusting my mother's wheelchair and my mother looked into her face and said, "What a pretty girl!" It was as if my daughter had gotten the gift of a lifetime. My daughter wanted everyone to know what my mother had said to her.

Sometimes, I took her to the mall, trying to re-create the childhood memories of our shopping trips. She seemed happy to be wheeled along the storefronts, browsing the merchandise and enjoying the purchases. Several memories stand out. One day, we dressed her in a lovely dress and a fashionable hat, and styled her hair. She took it all in, smiled at us, and sat taller in her wheelchair, looking confident and radiant. On another day, her independent spirit shone through as she ate her applesauce on her own at the table.

Those few instances and others like them, where my mother's true self appeared despite the Alzheimer's, are the memories we cherish.

There is a saying: "Enjoy the little things in life, because one day you'll look back and realize they were the big things." That rings so true to me. There is no greater love than to care for the one who brought you into this world. It's a gift that takes sacrifice, love, and an appreciation of the small wonders and miracles you have the good fortune to witness.

I lost my mother in 2017, but she still lives on in our hearts. The gift of taking care of her was the last and most precious gift she left us.

Maria Bynum is a 34-year federal government employee who has a passion for helping others professionally and through her organizational memberships with the Great Dames, Delta Sigma Theta Sorority, Inc. and The Links, Inc.

Confidence Redefined

By DeLores Pressley

My mother would tell me that I was her precious queen. "Stand tall. You are a beautiful girl," she would say when I worried about my height and weight. I was so blessed to have a mother who gave me such sustainable confidence. She set the tone for my life when I was at a very early age.

I wanted to be a ballerina more than anything in the world. My best friend and I would dance around our house and talk about being ballerinas. But the dance instructor would not allow my mother to sign me up for ballet because I was too fat. They let me take tap dance because they said it would help me lose weight. Of course, my best friend got the opportunity to take ballet lessons because she was reed-thin. Guess what? I always danced and actually took ballet lessons in my 60s.

Because of the values my mother instilled in me, I was able to overcome negative thoughts when I was told "no" to becoming a ballerina and felt the instructor was saying, "DeLores is not good enough." I had to consciously believe in myself and have confidence. Nearly 50 years later, I am still writing and talking about how all the "not good enough moments" in my life have made me become the person I am today.

During my junior year, I told my counselor at Timken Vocational

High School that I wanted to go to college. She reminded me that it was a vocational school, and I should learn a trade: "No, you are not here for college." Here we go again with "You are not good enough." I was devastated but that "no" was my avenue for growth. I graduated from the University of Akron with a teaching degree and taught third and fourth grades for 27 years.

I also wanted to be a model but was repeatedly rejected because society did not recognize plus women as models and no agency would take me seriously about being a professional. Once again, someone was saying, "You are not good enough," so I decided to create my own opportunity by creating the highly successful Dimension Plus Model Agency. Our clients ranged from Saks Fifth Avenue to *Glamour* Magazine and worked for the finest fashion houses and magazines in the world. This was nearly 30 years ago, so I guess you can say that I was a pioneer of the plus-size model fashion world.

Now I am a speaker, teacher, and confidence coach and have helped thousands of people live better lives. Oftentimes, I see people so inspired after hearing me speak that it nearly leaves me breathless. I touch people's lives and love what I do. I have been called a motivational speaker, but actually, I think the motivation comes from within you. I am merely a vehicle that relays something to an audience. The audience takes what I say, and it inspires them and moves them to action and a different level in their life. When I speak, it's from my heart, and I am gratified when I realize that others are inspired. I view it as a gift and am happy to be able to share it with others.

I encounter many people who say they are not where they want to be in their career, business, or life. I ask them to answer this question: "How can I overcome the rejections in my life that hold me back from realizing my goals and dreams?" This is what I know and teach. Your mind can play a major role in how you react and feel toward rejection. To "tap into your power," you need to learn why your mind takes you to places that will lead you off track on your journey.

On your way to discovering your true unconscious motivation and self-image, you definitely need patience to look at your unconscious actions, analyze them, and learn from them. But the reward is worth the labor. Through this process, you will be able to control your emotions and have a more correct, true and satisfying image of yourself.

How does self-consciousness play a part in tapping into your power? Sometimes, we are overly obsessive about how others observe us. When you are having negative self-consciousness about yourself, you are placing disapproving thoughts into your mind. Those unconstructive thoughts, such as doubt, will cause you to question your ability to do anything your heart desires. When you underestimate your value by processing pessimistic thoughts, you are placing a barrier between yourself and your true capabilities.

Having a low self-esteem will make you feel unworthy to others. You deserve better then to sabotage yourself with self-doubt! Take a risk and step outside of your comfort zone. Be courageous and have confidence in everything you do and achieve. Don't fall prey to the fear of failure. You are a worthy person and deserve to be successful.

I have a "Believe in the Power of You" jar. Each time that I accomplish something, I write it down and put it in the jar. It can be a small accomplishment like getting the opportunity to spend the day with my husband or a huge accomplishment like being the cover story for *Speaker* magazine. On the days that doubt tries to raise its ugly head, I immediately go to my jar and pull out one of my accomplishments. This gives me fuel to be motivated and know that I can accomplish anything.

So many times in my life, people have told me in one way or another that I am not good enough. I know different. I chose my beliefs. I chose to have positive beliefs. Had I allowed society to determine my self-worth, I would not be contributing to this book and living a life of success. Instead, I took what people meant to be a negative and turned it into a positive.

Love yourself enough to leave behind any habits or thoughts that hold you back. All your thoughts should lead you to the belief that you are good enough. And that is *Confidence Redfined*.

DeLores Pressley is an International Keynote Speaker, Author, Business Life Coach and Confidence Strategist with more than three decades of experience. She is President of DeLores Pressley Worldwide.

Stalker

By Jane Clark

I was 18 when I met Tom (probably not his real name) on social media before it was social media. He was somewhere out West, and we started a casual, virtual relationship. It was 2002 and webcams were all the rage. I used the opportunity to explore my sexuality and — you guessed it — send my nude photos to Tom.

After a few months, I met Rich. I really liked this guy and wanted to pursue a serious relationship, so I ended things with Tom. I didn't expect it to hurt him, since we had never met or even talked on the phone. Well, I must have hurt him, because he took revenge. Nuclear revenge.

He emailed my nudes to friends and co-workers. It was easy to find them on any social media site that shared my friends' list. Tom created online profiles on sites like MySpace and other platforms, posted my nudes as my profile pictures, and sent them to my circle of friends. He used my email address so I would get the messages from anyone who wanted to reach out. I was able to quickly take down the profiles and pictures he posted, but still ...

He even contacted Rich with a slanted cheating story. It certainly drove a wedge between us, but we weathered the storm. We dated for almost two years. We eventually broke up, but I still remember Rich fondly. Then

I fell in love with Todd, a college classmate. We had some photography classes together, and he made me laugh like no one else could. We were together a little over a year when I met Charles, who would eventually become my greatest love.

Meanwhile, Tom was still spreading gossip about me — it continued for years. Yes. Years. Four years, to be exact. *"Looks like Jane is turning a new leaf,"* he said to a friend who shared the message with me. He wouldn't let it go. However, he blocked me so I could not contact him directly. He only communicated with people in my circle. I was at his mercy for four terrifying long years, always looking over my shoulder and waiting for the other shoe to drop. I reported one of the email accounts he used to stalk me, and it was deactivated. I thought he might leave me and my friends alone. A small victory, but a catalyst.

Then came the grand finale when I was 22. I remember exactly what I was wearing when my dad called me. I was in the Walmart parking lot in a navy-blue tank top with white polka dots and a white pleated skirt. I also remember feeling brave that day and wearing some rather provocative tights. I was about to go on my first date with Charles, my now husband.

"You need to come home," Dad said. I knew he knew. I hoped he didn't, but somewhere deep down I knew he knew. I drove home, a bunch of frogs tumbling in my stomach. He was on the deck as I climbed up the stairs. He was very quiet, which meant this was serious. "So how long have you been using your camera as a webcam?"

There. There it was. The feeling sank really low down somewhere into a compartment I didn't know I had. My father was so disappointed in me. Mad at me. I was a whore, after all, right?

Tom had done his research. He bought my information online. The envelope was sent to my current address, and the return address was my previous home, where I hadn't lived for many years. He wanted to ensure this was received. In the letter addressed to my father, he said I needed help and that I was stalking him, and asked my father to tell me to leave him alone. He also included all our sexy conversations and all the nudes I had sent him to spin his narrative. It was true, though. I had said all those things and sent him all those photos.

The worst thing? The envelope was mailed from the state I lived in. Although I had some ideas about who the stalker was, I did not know who it was for certain. Tom was probably just a personality they created to converse with me. This Tom didn't really exist.

I told my dad the whole story. I told him how we had an online fling almost four years ago, that I ended things, and this must be his last and final act. Ideally. My dad was worried about my sister, who is six years my junior, and afraid this creep would attack her or me. He made me talk to my sister to ensure she knew that I "wasn't an example" so she'd "never do what I did." Then he told me to take the envelope and go to the police station. Alone. He also told me to change my clothes. Something less slutty, I guess.

I got in my Jeep and drove to the station with my nudes in hand. A male officer was there to greet me. When he looked at what I handed him, he brought in a female officer. The process was disheartening. Back then, they didn't really have the technology to find out who this guy was, and technically he didn't break the law. All they did was take my dad's and my fingerprints to exclude us. They would call if they found anything, but they didn't even run the prints, because, according to the officer, it wasn't a high enough priority.

In an effort to protect me, my dad put me on lockdown. He restricted my computer access. I had to come straight home from work, only being allowed to exercise and go to church. I normally didn't do either and I was absolutely miserable. I found refuge with my friends, but otherwise I hid under the biggest boulder, afraid to talk to anyone. Were they the stalker? Who had I hurt so badly that they thought I deserved this?

It was my lowest point. Thinking of Charles kept me sane. Technically,

What have I learned from all of this?

- You aren't the bad things that happen to you. I don't identify as someone society may think of as a sexual deviant, and my friends always had my back. As the wise Maya Angelou said, "When we know better, we do better."
- You aren't responsible for the actions of other people. It's not your fault. *Period.*
- Don't make decisions out of fear. Don't hide. Don't let them win. Don't let these bad experiences we call life prevent you from being vulnerable and authentic with those who deserve it.
- Own it. In the end, I'll probably never run for president, but there will always be a photo album in cyberspace of me looking ravishing in my heyday.
- Find the lightheartedness in every moment. Hundreds of movies bring comedic relief to this very issue.

Jane Clark helps her clients break away from the flock as a brand and marketing strategist with over 15 years of experience and a dozen first-place awards.

20-20 Hindsight

By Jill Slader-Young

Life and classic comic book origin stories are a bit different. Good guys and bad guys aren't always obvious. Happy endings don't always occur. Gray areas exist all over and can induce confusion. 20-20 hindsight is real and quite revealing.

I started my life as the only child of two baby boomer parents who did the best with what they had, both emotionally and experientially. My father was a sniper in the Marines who shifted those skill sets into running security for a major car manufacturer. My mother was a secretary for a major real estate agent who started straight out of high school and then shifted into being a stay-at-home mom on my arrival 10 years into their marriage.

My parents provided me with what I now recognize as a privileged existence. I had a home in a friendly, working-class neighborhood, homemade meals were always on the table, bills were always paid, and I benefited from a private school education. We vacationed on a regular basis. My father owned a boat and would take me fishing and crabbing on the Chesapeake. I was lucky.

Despite all these advantages, I struggled to understand why I elicited harsh reactions from my mother during childhood (and adulthood). I was a straight-A student who never got into trouble but was always being scolded, yelled at, insulted, and mocked. My interpretation of her actions was that I was bad. Something about me was not good enough. Jill must be a problem.

My father would do what he could to shield me but found himself in situations where he was trying to placate his wife and emotionally protect his daughter — between a rock and a hard place. I did not know until after she died that my mother *never* dreamed of being a mother. She had other hopes and dreams for her life that did not include the title of Mom. I internalized the notion that I was a problem and needed to try my best to be the perfect daughter. My inner critic saw all faults and flaws, never recognizing any assets or gifts.

At 7 years old, I proved to be a natural athlete, to my parents' delight. My parents were thrilled. My father had been a baseball player in his youth and my mother felt robbed of sports opportunities because of the time she grew up in as a girl. 20-20 perspective comes into play again here. My mother was living vicariously through me and my father was seeing a reflection of himself within his daughter.

My sophomore year in high school, this all changed. I woke up one morning and could not stand. The pain was excruciating, and my mother quickly made a doctor's appointment with an orthopedic specialist. I was taken to the hospital, stretched like an inanimate object on a slab and x-rayed. It was my spine: herniated disks, a birth defect, and scar tissue galore. I was in and out of physical therapy, while tending to academics and searching for a new title to replace "athlete." I found it in "girlfriend."

Unfortunately, I was naïve, which made me susceptible to one particularly less-than-healthy relationship that would continue on and off for more years than I care to admit. I hid any abuse that occurred because I certainly did not want to taint my "perfect daughter" title.

This continued into college. 20-20 perspective now informs me that I was preyed upon because of my personality type, self-perceived flaws, and need to please. My issues with self-esteem made me a target.

Next up for me was college. My parents were elated. Neither had gone to college, so I was a first in my family. When you are a first, there is no book of knowledge to benefit from, so I tried my best. Freshman year, I majored in education, maintained good grades, and fostered friendships. My spine issues were manageable. I felt relatively good about myself.

This continued into my sophomore year until the end of spring semester, when I was raped. I will not provide details of this experience; I will only say that it changed me, and I still resent that change. However, with 20-20 perspective, I recognize that I have learned a tremendous amount from being a survivor, and it has provided me with a lifetime mission to make a difference. I never wanted anyone to go through what I did.

In the aftermath of that trauma, I found a safe place with a haven of a human being who, at the time, never knew how much he aided in gluing me back together. I loved and cherished his vulnerability when we were together. I had zero fear of him. However, we just couldn't seem to make a relationship work. My 20-20 perspective informed me that there is a time and place for every person in your life, and traumas can interrupt the best of connections.

My senior year had its challenges, including partial, temporary paralysis and spine surgery. I was a 21-year-old with a walker, just trying to finish my degree and maintain some semblance of personal dignity. I graduated and made my parents proud. My 20-20 hindsight tells me that I learned, grew, changed, and endured for a bigger purpose than I was aware of at that time in my life. I was not yet willing to acknowledge my successes because I was still an individual with tremendous self-doubt and low sense of worth.

I became a teacher and professionally, I wanted to make sure that every young person I interacted with felt seen, valued, appreciated, protected, and cherished for their uniqueness. This was a mission I took seriously and sank my soul into every single day, for years. 20-20 hindsight tells me now that I was trying to right the wrongs I experienced as a child. I was trying to save all the "Jills" out there in the world. I was still carrying some very toxic guilt with me.

I then met someone older than me, and kinder than I recognized other men to be. He was a gentler being who wanted nothing more than to care for me and protect me. Shortly after entering this relationship, I had a complete and utter breakdown. I had held so many things at bay for so long that my mind and my body got together and said, "Enough. You need time to heal." I was making the best decisions I could with the knowledge base I had. I also got married.

Looking back with that wonderful 20-20 hindsight, I can clearly see the C-PTSD tsunami that was approaching me at the time. I see its purpose and appreciate the reset it provided. It was a somatic gift from the miraculous machine of one's self. However, it was quite a hell to endure, but I had a deep appreciation for the companion who stood by my side.

After some time, I ushered healthy twin sons into the world and felt phenomenal. In my mind, I was going to love, protect, guide, and save them from all the trauma I had gone through. I was going to apply the entire personal and professional book of knowledge I had gathered thus far to cocoon them in a safe space constructed for thriving. I did a relatively good job of this with pitfalls in patience at times, but I was proud of my parenting. 20-20 hindsight now shows me that I neglected myself and my husband by submerging completely into motherhood and teaching in attempts to save my sons and all the children I was guiding professionally.

The pressure increased when my father was diagnosed with stage 4 colon cancer. I was devastated. I added caretaker to my roles until my father died just before my sons' fifth birthday. One year later, my mother was diagnosed with breast cancer, and I found myself right back on the hamster wheel. 20-20 hindsight shows me now that I was floundering. I needed help. I needed to speak up and say, "I CAN'T KEEP DOING ALL THIS AND BE OKAY!"

Sadly, the me I was then didn't have it in her. My marriage fell apart. My sense of self dissolved. My soul cracked. My mother passed, and I went into an existential crisis because now I was an orphan.

I can also now see that I did not process my grief for either of my parents at all. I just kept moving forward. Luckily, I reconnected with that beautiful, safe haven of a human being who stands by my side loving me, supporting me, and cheering me on. He knew who "Jill" was. He could truly see me, and I borrowed strength from that precious gift. It helped me grow incredibly and I was given opportunities to travel, return to school, shift careers, and rediscover who I was. I set out to heal others.

With the help of my new husband, I started a nonprofit to serve survivors of sexual assault, domestic violence, and rape. Safe Haven Healing gave me a means to advocate for those I identified with: survivors who needed a safe space.

20-20 hindsight has shown that I still had healing to do myself. I was fully capable of serving others in a caring and ethical manner, but I was headed toward being a dry well because by this time I was carrying so many roles, with so many titles: Wife. Mom. Stepmother. Trauma Counselor. Business Partner. Doctoral Student. Daughter-in-Law. Ex-Wife. Co-Parent. Survivor. No one can carry that many titles successfully. Some of those balls are going to be dropped in the juggling act. And I started dropping balls. The kryptonite of being a superhero—of doing it all—was starting to affect my well-being.

Today, I am still dropping balls, but I pick them right back up and keep juggling to the best of my capabilities. I am actively constructing my own hierarchy of needs to manage my life better now. I am acknowledging and processing all the grief and trauma that has helped form my inner strength. I am mindfully expressing gratitude for everything that has occurred in my life because without it, I wouldn't have my superpower:

my 20-20 hindsight.

This power permits me to relate to a myriad of people. It gives me the gift of a book of knowledge and volume of empathy that makes helping others a natural act. My origin story gives me the power that drives my desire to change the world through helping other human beings. I am not here to save people. I am here to *help* people. And I know I can because I already have and will continue to do so, for the remainder of my story.

Jill Slader-Young is a trauma therapist. She is the founder and executive director of Safe Haven Healing, Inc. – a non-profit working with survivors of sexual assault, domestic violence, and rape.

A Sense of Belonging

By Annum Nashra

As a kid, I never felt like I fit in anywhere, so I created and lived in my own little world. I made an "art store" out on my grandmother's balcony when I was only six years old. I would color on paper and sell my art to my generous family members who bought them even when I colored out of the circle (which I mostly did).

"Too mature for her age" is a statement I would hear almost every day when growing up. As a teenager, I started volunteering at different organizations and teaching because I loved the idea of being able to create change. A moment of my life that I think has had the most impact was when I was in high school and joined a leadership program for college women: the World Academy for the Future of Women (WAFW).

When I met Jerrie Ueberle, the founder of WAFW, I knew my life was going to change forever. WAFW is a bold and daring leadership program that aims to develop future women leaders worldwide and operates in China, Bangladesh, Nepal, and the USA. WAFW wasn't like any other leadership program I'd experienced because it required a commitment of eight to 10 hours every day for an entire year.

I was not seen as too mature for my age at WAFW. My skills and perspectives about the world were nurtured and appreciated. This only inspired me to keep going. One of my facilitators, Bridget Kelly, visited my hometown in Bangladesh to teach us a module. After she returned to the United States, she reached out and invited me to join Great Dames events. I jumped at the opportunity because Great Dames provided a safe place for me to be myself and connect with some of the most phenomenal women I know.

Soon after, I saw a Great Dames social media post that requested applications for a four-year full scholarship to Wilmington University in Delaware. I applied for this incredible opportunity and was awarded the scholarship. Now, I was going to college in the States and I was beyond excited to explore this opportunity!

I completed my first year online in Bangladesh and moved to Delaware for the rest of my degree.

Fast-forward 10 months: I now work as a career services assistant at Wilmington University while maintaining a full academic schedule. I was also a WAFW delegate at the UN headquarters in March of this year and am helping to expand WAFW in different corners of the world. The past few months of my life have been filled with traveling, meeting new people, and learning new things. I absolutely love the way I am getting to experience life right now.

Although I still have a long way to go, the one thing I've learned so far is that as long as you move forward in life with pure intentions and love in your heart, opportunities will find a way to reach you. And you will discover a way not only to fit in, but to lead.

Annum Nashra is student at Wilmington University, DE, who was born in Dhaka, Bangladesh and aims to conquer the world.

.

we weren't allowed to date since we worked at the same company, so he quit. We played "Magic the Gathering" online, and I saw him face to face when I could. I told him everything and he never ran away. We became inseparable and have been married for 15 years.

My father did come around after a month or so. I remember breaking down when he finally could look at me and meet my eyes. He didn't want this guy to win. He knew I was the victim and deserved support. After that, he never brought it up again. He never made me feel badly about what happened or what I did. If this had happened today, I know my father would handle things differently. I had four years to process what happened, but he was just then going through all the stages of my anxiety in a very short amount of time. He's mellowed out in his old age and today we make light of what happened.

One good thing did come from my father finding out: The worst-case scenario had happened. I was free. The stalker no longer had any power over me.

With today's smartphones, this is far from a unique story. Yet, I truly believe we're on the cusp of something as a society. Instead of saying to the woman, "Wow, you're dumb for sending those pictures," we say to men, "Wow, you're cruel and pathetic for doing this." For several generations, sex had been taboo...for women. Women had to cover up so we wouldn't tempt a man. To sleep around was shameful for women, but something to boast about for men. Carry your keys in your hand when you enter the parking lot. Look around for danger. Don't wear that low-cut shirt — you'll be asking for it.

Now, we tell men it's not acceptable to hurt women. It's not okay to rape women, no matter what they're wearing. It's not okay to distribute private photos of your partner after a breakup. Revenge porn is shameful. It's not okay to use vulnerability as ammunition in any parting-of-the-ways.

Navigating Life Through Fiction

By Debbra A.K. Johnson

My life has always fallen between fact and fiction. Fiction was a friend, serving me well. It allowed me to envision and experiment who I could be. When I was young, I created and embellished my families' pasts to create scenarios where I could live in the skin of a different set of circumstances—try them on, mold them and discard them when they were no longer of use.

Given my vivid imagination, richly fed by movies and television shows of the '50s and '60s, the world seemed a playful, challenging, and wondrous place. My fictions were my shield, providing rays of hope that allowed me to not only have a plan, but believe that I could achieve that plan and someday be educated and capable with a full, meaningful, and useful life.

Facts were often my enemy. Broken homes and life in trailers, housing projects, and places on the wrong side of the tracks until I left home at 17. There was a philandering father and a mother who was tortured by her own life's circumstances, and later we found that she had a severe learning disability. All this and more were the conditions that defined me to the world, and the world was not kind.

I credit my use of fiction to providing the ability to see, feel, and process quickly and completely. While useful personally, it has been a key aspect of my professional life. I fictionalize things or visualize and play out what these things could mean. Because of this ability, my ideas and decisions tend to be clear and fast.

After graduating at the bottom of my high school class, I graduated magna cum laude from college. I also had a leg up when I entered the workforce: I'd already worked in the retail, tourism, restaurant, manufacturing, supermarket, healthcare, printing, and the newspaper businesses. My work study jobs helped build my writing, research, typing, and photography skills. Now it was time to put these facts to good use in my next set of fictions.

My first professional job out of college was as a public relations coordinator for a hospital. Within the first few months there, an opportunity came my way. I attended a program offered by United Airlines to teach people about the group dynamics and human behaviors that can get in the way of successfully working together. A couple weeks afterward, the CEO of our hospital asked if I could facilitate the program at the hospital. Although I had no background in training and facilitation, I fictionalized myself into the role and saw it clearly.

What I saw was the performance of exposing others to new ideas, and I knew I could do a good job. If nothing else, I'd entertain our way through it. This was also meaningful and useful work—creating an environment where people could work together more effectively, efficiently, and respectfully, and helping reduce the hesitations, holding back, and second-guessing that cause stress. I fictionalized the scenarios where people's lives could actually be affected positively, and lives could even be saved.

I continued to have a rich career using my fictionalizing method. For example, I helped a semiconductor company win a major contract for the Trident missile. In helping with the presentation, I fictionalized who would be in the room, what they wanted to hear, what would be important to them, what questions would they ask, what would convince them to select us, and what would push them away.

Joining a major insurance company, I learned about audio-video production. This was the richest and largest platform suitable for me to fictionalize yet. We took this new tech to places it hadn't been before, from the development of AV-rich training products to the use of complex programmed multi-image recognition shows that honored our top brokers and agents.

When the company decided to go public, it was clear that my ability to climb in the organization was extremely limited, even though I had been rated one of the company's top performers. The facts overwhelmed any chance of fictionalizing the situation. It was time to take stock of my career and fictionalize what was next.

My husband and I formed an integrated marketing company. After building the business up to a healthy client base, it was hit hard by the merger and acquisition frenzy of the '90s. A sports apparel client offered me a corporate position, and I rose to director of international marketing. By that time, I had worked for nearly every major employer in Maine and wanted to seek opportunities with multinationals. That meant looking outside the state.

I joined DuPont in 1998, and the job was perfect. Everyone was involved in one way or another in fictionalizing the future. My break came when our CEO started talking about sustainability. I was hooked from the start. I began diving into everything and anything I could read about the topic and by mid-2006, I had an idea of how to apply sustainability to our business. That work opened up other opportunities.

In 2010, I was asked to represent the company with the UN Office of Disaster Risk Reduction, which was setting up a private sector group. The organization works at the intersection of disaster risk reduction, resilience, and sustainability—the kind of things that are complex and unknown: a perfect sweet spot. It had always been one of my far-off musings to be seated at the UN in some capacity. My education and life hadn't been on that track, so I never fully fictionalized it, but here it was.

You'd think that after a 50-year career, the opportunities to fictionalize would melt away. Not so. Instead, there are more opportunities than ever, so the journey continues. The use of fictions has brought opportunities to learn, to connect, do, and increase the levels of capabilities and confidence. In turn, these lead to more opportunities for better fictions and the possibilities to do more and more useful and meaningful work, influencing and having an impact on things that matter.

There are many inspiring quotes for this, from Mahatma Gandhi's "be the change you want to see" to R. Buckminster Fuller's "be the architects of the future, not its victims." What both these recognize is that the world is interconnected: It's a system of systems, where each of us can play a role. In some cases, the facts of the thing or situation may immediately connect with you. In other cases, it might be a stretch but, in all cases, fictionalizing or envisioning that role and its impact, is a power-giving and way-finding approach.

When we view things put before us through this lens, it helps us explore their importance to us and seek our place within them without fear or hesitation. We can find and define ourselves and/or powers within them. This way of thinking is the air and water needed to fictionalize, imagine, or envision the thing and your role in it. Life can become a series of experiments that build on each other, enabling us to be the change and the architect of those things that deliver meaning and fulfillment.

Debbra A.K. Johnson is a resilience advisor, collaboration broker, and lifelong learner who specializes in complex issues and 'wicked problems.'

Walking My Brother Home

By Dian O'Leary

My brother died on December 31. His wife, Denise, came down the stairs from where he had been sleeping for three days and said through muted tears, "Alan died a few minutes ago." A year and a half since being diagnosed with a brain tumor (a glioblastoma), my youngest brother would tell no more jokes, would not call at odd hours to say "I love you," would not hug me or his son or his wife or his brother or his sisters again. I still miss him.

That night, for the first time in a month, I packed my bags and left my brother's family's home. I had been there to help them walk him home in peace, the lightning rod for the emotions and tensions Alan and Denise and Tyler cycled through, knowing that in a week, two weeks, a month at most, Alan would leave them.

I traveled the six hours from my home in Delaware to Alan's house in Pittsburgh in early December after my sister Joanne called me at work to tell me that Denise and Tyler were afraid to stay in the house with Alan because he would light a cigarette on the gas burners and then forget to turn them off, and they were afraid to leave him alone. Denise, a pharmacist, needed to work to keep her health insurance and my 12-year-old nephew Tyler needed to go to school.

My boss happened to be sitting next to me when I took the call and she said, "Go. Just go. We'll figure something out." I left the next day.

My sister was at Alan's house when I arrived and transferred my funeral clothes to her car. I inflated a beige air mattress, on loan from a friend, in their family room, which was to be my bedroom for the next month. Inflating it made quite the racket and Tyler bounced and slid and tumbled and giggled, and we joined him, grateful for the relief.

Denise and Tyler headed out the next day and I set up my computer on the kitchen table so I could work. Alan watched TV in the adjacent living room, or used the treadmill in the basement, or lifted weights, or did his sit-ups. My brother did 100 sit-ups on December 26, the day before he lapsed into a coma. Glios affect everyone differently and we were fortunate to have Alan as we knew him up until the tumor grew into his brain stem. Most people are not as fortunate.

Settling into a routine, I worked at the kitchen table most of the morning, then joined Alan on the couch to watch MeTV. We held hands and watched "Wagon Train," "The Andy Griffith Show," "The Rifleman," and I'm pretty sure we saw a few "Lassies". I still can't watch those shows. I can watch "Titanic" and "It's a Wonderful Life," though, two more classics we watched many times, and that Alan could recite by heart. "What is it you want, Mary? What do you want? You want the moon? Just say the word, and I'll throw a lasso around it and pull it down."

Joanne and our niece, Jessica, came out one afternoon and we made the Christmas cookies my mom always made: molasses sugar cookies, spritz cookies with glittery decorations, nut rolls, nut horns, kolaches ... so many cookies.

Alan's many friends, along with my brother Jeff and his wife Arlene, visited regularly. He related one nighttime visit from our long-dead maternal grandmother and described her dog, Wrinkles. Alan was born after Wrinkles died. My brother did not die alone.

He would plead, "I don't want to go away. I don't want to go away. I

276

want to stay with Tyler." I felt my heart recede in my chest, hiding from his pleas and my grief. I didn't want him to go away either and we both knew we had no power and no choice.

Another time, he said, "I don't want to go to bed. I don't have many nights left and I don't want to miss one." I had been listening to Wayne Dyer tell a story about his daughter and I channeled him, saying, "If I thought that staying up all night would help you feel better, I would sit here all night with you. But it won't. You'll just be tired tomorrow when you will want to be with Denise and Tyer." He cocked his head, went up the stairs to bed, and slept all night.

I visited about once a month after Alan's diagnosis and would stay at Joanne's house. At first, we went to the local mall to window shop or to Target for supplies. The whole family went once to Olive Garden for dinner. I was able to eat, but I felt empty inside as I watched my brother's hands shake as he lifted his fork. Later on, I would stop at a Dunkin' Donuts, bring back donuts and coffee for the family, and then we would get in the car and drive around town for hours, sometimes jabbering and sometimes in silence. He had me take him to where he and Jeff used to fish and he said, "I wish we could fish here again next summer."

We went grocery shopping one afternoon and he ran into a former co-worker. She complained about their employer and her job. When we got in the car, he said, "I wish I could complain about something as simple as my job. People don't know what they have."

I went to the same local mall to do some holiday shopping. I felt so lonely there without my brother to look at the little glass figurines that my mother loved so much when she was alive. I also felt short-lived relief to be away from the house. I didn't know I needed that.

I went out one more time before he died to buy some new glasses and use up my Flexible Savings Account money. He asked me to stop at a local shop and get him a roast beef hoagie. I got there at 5 p.m. and they were closing up shop, and all I could get was an Italian hoagie. I'm still sad that

I couldn't get that damned roast beef hoagie.

I did make my brother's last meal, as it turned out. I had used the Christmas chicken carcass to make soup stock and was planning to make chicken and dumplings the next day. Alan said, "What are you waiting for?" I made it that night and the four of us — Alan, Denise, Tyler, and I — ate my chicken and dumplings.

The next morning, Alan fell when he tried to get out of bed. His legs wouldn't hold him. I held him up so he could use the bathroom and he fell back into bed. I called Denise at work and said, "You need to come home now." She did. He tried that afternoon to rise; with me taking his torso and her his legs, we lifted him back into bed.

Alan died three days later. Denise and Tyler needed to be alone, so at 11:30 that night, I packed up and went to my sister's house, spent and deeply grateful for that month with my brother.

It's been 10 years and I still ache when I think of Alan. He brought affection to our stoic Irish Catholic family, hugging us in greeting, saying "I love you" just out of the blue. He also was a mess. He's the guy who would come home on Christmas Eve with all of his gifts needing to be wrapped a half hour before our family's traditional party started. Once he was married, that continued. By then, though, he was also the guy who channeled Chevy Chase in "Christmas Vacation," decorating his house with thousands of lights and every inch of his yard with inflatable Santas and reindeers and Pooh Bears. That was our littlest bro.

I'm also still grateful for the honor of being Alan's sister and his friend. I learned how to sit still and not try to fix anything. I learned how to let him be and feel and do what he needed to do when he needed to be or feel or do it. I was able to love him the way he wanted to be loved. I try to remember to "know what I have" and be grateful that at least today, my complaints and distractions are simple ones.

I learned, too, that we don't have to do any of this alone. My boss and my co-workers picked up my slack for more than a month. Yes, I worked.

No, I was not very productive. My dear friend Mae and her husband hosted me to watch the Steelers-Browns game, so I had someplace to go. We hardly talked and that was OK.

I know I have been blessed and changed by helping Denise and Tyler walk my brother home. And I still wish I could answer the phone and hear him say, "I just called to tell you I love you."

Dian O'Leary is a writer who transforms complex ideas into relatable narratives, fostering understanding, dialog, and collective action.

The Healing Journey

By Taylor Urban

You have cancer.

These are words no one wants to hear. I never expected to hear them on a cold January afternoon in 2021. I was 45 years old, active, healthy, no symptoms, and no family history. How many times I'd heard people say they couldn't believe it happened to them, but sometimes bad things just happen for no reason at all. That is a mystery of life.

Rewind a couple months earlier. COVID had rocked me. I didn't imagine much more could happen or that I could survive. Mandated closure of my retail business. My kids' schools closed. The stress and anxiety of navigating all things COVID. There were days I felt my heart was in a vise because I was so overwhelmed.

I started praying more and learning deep breathing exercises in desperation and trying to cope. I didn't think it could get much worse ... and then I got a surprise cancer diagnosis.

The good news: I survived. They found my cancer early, during a routine mammogram, and it was very treatable Stage 1. The breathing and prayer practices I had started because of stress helped me so much during those early days after my diagnosis. It's funny how things like that happen at just the right times in our lives. Serendipity.

The bad news: My cancer was spread out, and a mastectomy was my best course of action. I had "areas of concern" in my other breast, which would put me at high risk for future occurrences. I elected for a bilateral mastectomy with reconstruction and committed to putting cancer behind me and take my life back.

I remember being amazed after I was diagnosed that the birds kept chirping and the sun shone while people like me had cancer. That a heart could break while another finds joy.

I went from healthy to mastectomy with reconstruction in about three months. Everyone was amazed at how I got through it because it all happened so fast. In some ways, the surgery and treatment were the easy parts. You're in fight-or-flight mode. You put on a brave face for your loved ones, and you just keep moving.

People would say I was so brave and inspired them with my journey. Mostly, I was just trying to inspire myself. I felt like I needed to be strong for them to know I'd be okay. The funny thing about being brave is you often don't know you're doing it until after you've done it. Looking back, I *was* brave.

What I didn't realize was the bravest thing would not be surviving cancer but choosing to live my best life. There is no right or wrong way to be a survivor, and it took me awhile to learn that. Many days, I felt the hoorah of survivorship — a pink warrior, strong, brave, beautiful; you name it! I laughed in the face of death and cancer. Other days, I'd sob in the shower, asking, "Why me?"

One day, I cried in my yoga class out of mourning and frustration about not being able to do a pose because of tightness from my surgery. My body is different now and that is just hard to accept. It is such a roller-coaster and so very few get it. It was in accepting that dichotomy and connecting with other survivors that my survival story and healing journey really began.

I have to be honest. My moment of reckoning came with the gentle nudge of my childhood best friend, telling me I needed a therapist. She didn't know what to say, but she knew I was not in a good place. I was lost, broken, and trying to navigate my life as a breast cancer survivor. I would tell everyone I was fine, grateful to be alive, but a good friend always knows what stirs beneath the surface.

Like many people, my life moved so fast before cancer, I was so damn busy. I was both stressed and blessed. I grew up on Long Island, went to college in Delaware, married my next-door neighbor, and had three beautiful children with him. My husband and I ran our own retail business. Beyond work and family, I didn't have a whole lot of time or energy left. I thought this was what happens to all of us: You put your life on pause during these middle-age parenting years.

Or do you? During my recovery, I read a lot of books about cancer, self-help, meditation, and trauma. I searched every nook and cranny, looking for answers to fix the broken parts of my heart. I was supposed to be grateful to be alive. Why wasn't I happy now? Was it the cancer that made me feel this ache? Was it my mortality? Will I get sick again? Is this my fault? Will living with my new body ever feel normal?

And the biggest question we all ask: What have I done with my life? Is this my legacy? I wrote my obituary during this time and announced to my therapist that I just didn't like it well enough. That was when I began to "do my work," as one my favorite authors, Brene Brown, would say. I told my best friend that I thought I needed to "get a life."

I started exploring and remembering the little girl I once was. I went down some rabbit holes to better understand the story of my youth. I had some difficult conversations with family and friends. Some boundaries got reset, and although I hate to say, I even let some bridges crumble. I decided I was going to mother and honor that little girl I once was. I was going to heal and live my best life.

I learned to be present. I started to focus on the moments in my life, be present for them, and capture them in my heart, mind, and journal.

I decided to go to more concerts and be the one having the most fun singing and dancing. I saw remarkable things during that time that made many people wonder. I felt God's presence, my angels, loved ones past in my life. Some things were so far out of my comfort zone, and some things were easy.

I learned it's okay to get sad, mourn, and grieve, and that I needed to sit with those parts of me. That trauma awakens trauma and is a spirally and weird place to get out of. The secret was not to stay there too long. Grief is not a life sentence. Pain hurts but won't destroy me. Time heals.

I developed a toolbox of things that refueled me and did my best to return to those when life would overwhelm me. I slowly learned to ask for help. To love myself for the beautiful and broken mess I could be. No matter the weather, I had her back. I'd silence the *shoulds*.

That first summer after my surgery, I joined a volunteer group for women. When I was growing up, volunteering was something I really enjoyed, but I had gotten away from it once I became a parent. It seemed school and sports activities got all my energies, but my community, not so much. Joining that group was a step toward the person I used to be — the girl who wanted to change the world and be a helper.

The next thing I did was connect with the Delaware Breast Cancer Coalition (DBCC.) I got trained as a peer mentor to support other women who had been diagnosed. I needed purpose in my pain, and since I shared my story pretty openly, I had a lot of people come to me for help. I had high school friends message me privately that they had been diagnosed and told no one. I was grateful that I could help them, and they trusted me enough to come to me for support.

The best part of DBCC has been the friendships, love, and support that I've gotten from this remarkable group of women. The survivor events and resources they have for us. I am eternally grateful for all they have done and continue to do for me, my survivor sisters, and our community.

I started playing guitar and tried to accept I was bad at it. We grownups aren't very good at being bad at things. I signed up for a yoga class and chose more scenic spots to walk the dog when I realized I really don't like walking the neighborhood every day. Nature and trails made my dog and me happy. My mom had been a writer, and I hadn't written much since her death nearly 25 years ago. I bought a pretty journal and I started to write again. Now I journal almost every day and I love it. It's my special time by the window with my coffee each morning.

I guess the moral of this story is that surviving cancer wasn't really my brave moment. My brave moment came when I decided how I wanted my life to be and committed to that. I feel more alive and more myself than I have in years. My circle stood by me, and I met some amazing new friends along the way. This journey will be mine now for the rest of my days. It's not always easy, but it's my best authentic life right now, which I will absolutely take over the fly-by existence I had before.

Brave is stepping up and promising myself I will do my best for me. I deserve the sun and the moon, and I will spend each day making the best of this sweet life.

Taylor Urban is a breast cancer survivor, mother, wife, sister, friend, daughter, dreamer, writer, and nature lover. Taylor runs Urban Furniture Outlet with her husband, following a career as a mental health and school counselor.

Racing Through Open Doors

By Judith Luther-Wilder

Will Durant said that "vanity increases with age." He also viewed the memoir he wrote with his wife, Ariel, as an act of vanity. While 10-page tales about "great dames" will never tell the whole story of a life and can hardly be called memoirs, the philosopher/author of *The Story of Civilization* might view even one 10-page entry written for a Great Dames book as a first step on the Road to Vanity. If not Hell. Still, with no disrespect to other contributors to Great Dames' publications, it is probably safe to say we will not be judged by the rigorous standards imposed on Presidential Medal of Freedom authors.

That said, where to begin and what to include in 10 autobiographical pages that may be scrutinized by discerning readers with a keen eye for bullshit and puffery? Since I am a big fan of "less is more," I may aim for four or five rather than 10 pages and skip the travelogue that documents nickel-and-dime journeys from a small village in Nova Scotia to even smaller villages and a number of extraordinarily large cities in the USA, as well as China, Mexico, Europe, Asia, Australia, Africa, and New Zealand.

Given the entrepreneurial focus and flawless planning processes of most Great Dames, perhaps I should not spend too much time describing work in the arts, business, government, and the nonprofit world that was more accidental than by design.

Which, in fact, accounts for most of my life's work: So much of what I did over the years has been a function of being at the right place at the right time.

For example, when my second husband died, I was immediately given an opportunity to work in the Los Angeles Department of Recreation and Parks. I was neither trained for nor had ever considered a career in recreation. I had, however, volunteered for a number of programs at a sports and community center where my sons were involved in Little League and basketball programs. The director of Glassell Park Recreation Center suggested I test for a civil service position in recreation, and in what seemed like the blink of an eye, I was a certified recreation director for the City of Los Angeles. That led to employment in other departments and tours of duty in African American, Mexican American, Japanese, Chinese, Cambodian, and senior citizen communities. I was also offered opportunities to produce large arts festivals that miraculously attracted audiences of 100,000 to a million arts, sports, and fun lovers. Eventually, I was hired as superintendent of cultural affairs for the City of Long Beach.

As luck would have it, my future husband was then vice mayor of Long Beach and, as often happens, a professional relationship led to a personal partnership that then led, in 1981, to marriage.

Shortly after our backyard wedding, I resigned my position with the city and went to work for the United Cambodian Community, Inc. (UCC). At that time, Cambodian refugees represented 10 percent of the city's population and I became involved with local and overseas communities that included both the refugees in Long Beach and war-torn neighborhoods in Phnom Penh and Kampot. That experience included many trips to Southeast Asia and entrepreneurial training for amputees and widows, all of whom were struggling to survive in impoverished urban and rural areas of the country.

Those years changed my life in almost every important way.

During my many years of work with the Long Beach Cambodian community, I was often called to serve as a spokesperson for UCC. One evening when I was speaking at a local university, I met opera director Peter Sellars. On the following day, he contacted me and invited me to become the director of the Los Angeles Festival, the successor to the 1984 Olympic Arts Festival.

Although Sellars was still involved with the Glyndebourne Festival Opera and several other opera companies in Europe, he had also been recently appointed artistic director of the Los Angeles Festival. At that time (late 1980s), Peter, generally viewed as the *enfant terrible* of the opera community, was (and still is) a brilliant, charismatic figure in the American and European arts world. He had, I'm certain, already courted and been rejected by a dozen Los Angeles arts leaders he hoped would help him co-produce a $6 million citywide arts festival while he simultaneously managed his other global arts commitments.

In those days, $6 million was not viewed as chump change and since I had never administered more than a $1 million budget, I was duly impressed. While Peter doubtless approached me in a fit of desperation, I happily accepted the position. It was a hasty decision but a fortunate one. The experience turned out to be more fun than playing in the mud with a bunch of drunken monkeys during a monsoon wedding in Bali.

After the festival's orchestra played its last tune, I met the formidable Beatrice Fitzpatrick, who strong-armed me into taking a job with the New York-based American Women's Economic Development Corporation. The Small Business Administration's Women's Business Development Center (SBA WBDC) in Washington, D.C., then headed by Lindsey Johnson, funded our entrepreneurial training for California women businessowners. Lindsey is a miniature force of nature who became my business partner and lifelong friend. We eventually created Women Incorporated, a national nonprofit organization designed to finance and support women entrepreneurs.

Although we had talked about the development of a financial support organization for women entrepreneurs, Women Inc. didn't become a reality until we happened, again by chance, to meet Marc Turtletaub, owner of a financial institution called the Money Store. After a follow-up meeting with him in Sacramento, California, he agreed to give us $2 million to set up shop and develop a loan program for women businessowners. Within two months, we moved to Sacramento and were off and running.

A few years later, Lindsey decided to pursue an MBA at Harvard and I decided to return to Los Angeles to organize the Center for Cultural Innovation (CCI), a company that identified loans and financial support for independent (and entrepreneurial) artists. Cora Mirikitani, my CCI co-CEO, had vast experience as an arts producer and a philanthropic administrator. Together, we developed a series of lending and regranting programs for individual artists. That project still exists today, although it has evolved into a far more ambitious program than I ever envisioned.

Since those hectic days of working with women entrepreneurs, refugees, and independent artists, and after about 13 years of working on various programs for Sias International University (the first American Chinese university in China), I moved to Nova Scotia to enjoy more halcyon pursuits. These days, I write the occasional book and spend time with my husband, friends, and family members who also left California to put down new roots in this isolated and rustic Maritime community.

Although my travels to exotic and/or challenging places have been greatly curtailed by advancing years and a diminishing tolerance for discomfort, I continue to try to get back to Los Angeles or Hawaii at least every other year. My older son and his family still live in Southern California, and since so many close friends and calabash relatives still enjoy the excitement of urban living and sunshine far brighter than it is during most months in Nova Scotia, I will once again stuff a carry-on bag in May and head out for a month in Los Angeles. Since I expect the traffic, airport chaos, and general pace of L.A. will all be factors chasing me back to the brilliant summer and autumn sunsets over Point Prim and the Bay of Fundy near our cottage, I plan to return to my little haven on the cliff around the first of June. I imagine that upon my return, I will resume focusing a lot of energy and time in cyberspace in an ongoing effort to stay in touch with family and friends from another place and another time.

A good friend of mine once told me, "It's not true you can't have it all. You just can't have it all at once."

I think that's true. Looking back, I certainly haven't had it all, but I think I've had my share of whatever "all" is. Clearly I would love the Maritimes more if I could move all — no, most — family members and friends to Bay of Fundy communities, but on the other hand, absence *does* often make the heart grow fonder. I feel fortunate to remember most of my American kindred spirits vividly and to have lured many of them up here for short vacations. There have also been less satisfying, though more frequent, *visits*, courtesy of Zoom, and I appreciate the science (or magic) that allows me to gaze on familiar and beloved faces via technology.

I am also grateful to have shared my journeys hither and yon with so many extraordinary people, some of whom are members of my family and, with only one or two unfortunate exceptions, most of whom have enriched my life in wondrous ways. If only in small ways, I hope I have enriched theirs as well.

Every year or so, I receive delightful e-mails or letters from children I tutored during the Ice Age, around the time when my own sons were six and eight years old. They have found me on Facebook or somewhere in cyber space and write to reminisce about craft classes they attended at Verdugo Park Recreation Center or their favorite Rod Stewart album covers I used as tutoring tools. Of course, these *children* are now in their 60s and clearly are given to nostalgia and trips down memory lane. For adherents of living in the *now*, this may or may not be considered healthy.

That said, more than awards or false and inflated memories,

their childhood memories of making sand candles or learning to read florid blurbs on pop music album covers allow me to believe the impulsive decisions I made, with a few predictable and foolish exceptions, generally worked out extremely well. And for a few other high-stakes gamblers willing to bet on an eager but untested entity given to lying through her teeth whenever she said, "Sure, I can do that," I offer thanks.

I began this piece with a quote from a Will Durant essay and I will close it with a quote from another, albeit less esteemed, philosopher. Ferris Bueller said, "Life moves pretty fast. If you don't stop once in awhile, you could miss it." Another wag once told me, "It's better to be lucky than smart."

Although I haven't amassed a fortune, won a beauty contest, secured an Olympic medal, been tapped for a MacArthur Foundation genius grant, or enjoyed a ride on the Orient Express, I've been very, very lucky.

I also think I have come close (enough) to having it "all."

Judith Luther-Wilder is an author, a mother, grandmother, a refugee worker and a former LA City Arts Commissioner. She has traveled widely including to Vietnam, Cambodia, and Africa.

If It Were Possible, What Would I Do?

By Jerrie Ueberle

I was in Shanghai on one of many trips to China and finished my meetings early. I had three whole days before my return flight to the United States. Three days! Most people would not have seen that as a problem, but I am not good at relaxing or being a tourist.

I decided to fly to Japan and talk to others about the World Academy for the Future of Women, a program I founded and run to prepare young women and men for leadership roles that will address and achieve gender equality, social justice, and human dignity. I am constantly looking for supporters, facilitators, and new locations for the program that is currently in China, Nepal, and Bangladesh.

I booked a flight to Japan, had three fabulous days of meetings, and headed back to the airport for my return to Shanghai. When I gave the agent my ticket and passport, she informed me that I did not have a visa to return to China. She couldn't put me on the plane. I couldn't believe I had made that mistake. In those days, China only issued a single entry visa, not the 10-year one that is now available. I told her I needed to get back immediately to Shanghai to catch my flight back to the United States.

She said it was not possible. I would have to go to the Chinese consulate to get a visa, a process that would take three to five days.

I returned to Tokyo, booked a hotel for the night, and was ready to set out for the consulate. The concierge informed me that it was closed until the next morning, but regardless, it was absolutely impossible to get an entry visa in a day. Then I asked one simple question: *"If it were possible, what would I do?"* He thought a moment and gave me the name of a travel company. Unfortunately, the travel company validated what both the airline agent and concierge had said. It was impossible.

The next morning at 8 a.m., I took a taxi to the Chinese consulate. I dragged my luggage up three flights of stairs and once again was told getting an entry visa would take days. Again, I asked, *"If it were possible, what would I do?"* He told me to go sit in the waiting room and come back in two hours. Those were two long hours filled with uncertainty. When I returned to the desk, I said: "I'm here to pick up my visa." To my surprise, he handed me my passport with the visa inside.

I hailed a taxi and told the driver to please hurry to the airport because I had a flight. He explained it was impossible to get me there in rush hour traffic. Again I asked, *"If it were possible, what would I do?"* His advice was to take the fast train. It was a very hot day, but I started running and walking to the station. A woman on the street asked me where I was going in such a hurry and then grabbed one of my bags and ran with me to the train station.

The train was already there. If I went to purchase a ticket, I would miss my connection. I asked the woman who had run with me: *"If it were possible, what would I do?"* She told me to just get on the train without a ticket. I took off again at full speed and boarded. As I stood exhausted and sweating in the train, I looked over to see her passing a very cold Diet Coke to me through the window. The kindness of strangers.

When I got to the airport, the ticket agent told me that the flight had already boarded. For a final time, I asked: *"If it were possible, what would I* who has the opportunity to open a door that has not been open to you. It starts by asking: *"If It Were Possible, What Would I Do?"*

Jerrie Ueberle is the Founder/CEO of Global Interactions, a non-profit organization with consultative status with the United Nations. She created The World Academy for the Future of Women, a university level bold and daring program to accelerate the leadership of women worldwide in China, Nepal, and Bangladesh.

Great Dames
Call to Action

The world needs Great Dames.

Because Great Dames can change the world.

Reach out today to a woman or girl who might benefit

from a friendship, mentor, supporter, and advocate.

Tell her you believe in her.

Let her know her ideas are remarkable and worth hearing.

Encourage her to share her story.

Inspire her to be brave.

Learn more about the Great Dames global community:

www.GreatDames.com

Contact us: info@great-dames.com

Contact Our Storytellers

Carol Parkinson Arnold: cparnold35@yahoo.com

Pam Baker: www.linkedin.com/in/pamelawbaker

Wendy Battles: reinventionrebels.com/

Brad Beck: bradbeck220@icloud.com

Maria Bynum: www.linkedin.com/in/maria-bynum-83922123/

Jane Clark: www.linkedin.com/in/janeclark/

Beatrice "Bebe" Coker: bebecoker@gmail.com

Jah'Sima Cooper: Jayy1cooper@gmail.com

Carol Cunningham: Carol.d.cunningham@gmail.com

Cindy DelGiorno: WineTimeWithCindy@gmail.com

Gayle Dillman: www.linkedin.com/in/gayle-dillman-26335036/

Haverly Erskine: www.linkedin.com/in/haverlyerskine/

Lauren Foraker: www.linkedin.com/in/lauren-foraker-a4ab99148/

Robert Ford: mail@robertford.us

Lele Galer: galerfamily@comcast.net

Alison Garrett: www.linkedin.com/in/prisonbreakcoach/

Melissa Gonville: linkedin.com/melissa-k-gonville

Johnette Hartnett: johnettehartnett@gmail.com

Debbra A. K. Johnson: www.linkedin.com/in/debbra-j-5806b25/

Bridget Kelly: bkelly327@gmail.com

Sharon Kelly Hake: www.linkedin.com/in/sharonkellyhake/

Sarah Kenney-Cruz: www.linkedin.com/in/sarahkenneycruz/

Sara Beth Kohut: www.linkedin.com/in/sara-beth-kohut-84117598/

Geri Krolin-Taylor: gkrolintaylor@gmail.com

Flavia Loreto: www.flavialoretophotography.com

Gemma Lowery: www.linkedin.com/in/gemma-lowery-telehealth-advocacy

Judith Luther-Wilder: JudithALW@aol.com

Angela Marshall: angelamarshallmd.com/

Maureen McVail: Mmcvail@gmail.com

Annum Nashra: annumnashra07@gmail.com

Dian O'Leary: www.linkedin.com/in/dianoleary/

Alice Palokoff: ap3746@hotmail.com

Kathy Palokoff: www.linkedin.com/in/kathypalokoff/

DeLores Pressley: dp@delorespressley.com

Sindy Rodriguez: sinrod14@gmail.com

Andra Rush: www.linkedin.com/in/andra-rush-248a0671/

Patricia Russell: patricia31russell@gmail.com

Jennifer Ryan: ryanwall1813@yahoo.com

Sierra RyanWallick: sierra.ryanwallick@gmail.com

Mary Schreiber Swenson: www.linkedin.com/in/marysschreiberphd/

Jill Slader-Young: https://safehavenhealing.org/

Karen Smith: karensmithdrums.com

Nicolle D. Surratte: www.ahealthcoachforme.com

Mengdi (Mandy) Tao: www.linkedin.com/in/mandy-tao/

Taranna Tabassum Tiasha: www.linkedin.com/in/taranna-tabassum-tiasha-a24978198

Ruth E. Thaler-Carter: www.linkedin.com/in/ruthtcfreelancewritereditor/

Jerrie Ueberle: jerrie@globalinteractions.org

Giftie Umo: giftieumo@gmail.com

Taylor Urban: www.linkedin.com/in/taylor-urban-0433b57a/

Sue Weldon: www.uniteforher.org

Anna Welsh: littlebagsbyanna.com

Jan White: jansaysonward@gmail.com

Suzanne Zorn: can be reached through Great Dames at info@Great-Dames.com

Acknowledgments

Special thanks to our 52 remarkable storytellers who shared their powerful stories in this book. So many talented people supported this book project, and we are deeply grateful to them for taking this journey with us. Kathy Palokoff for her stellar editing and writing talents; Kelli Kilbride for her organizational powers; Maria Hess for reviewing and evaluating stories; Ruth Thaler-Carter for proofreading; and Jesse Baker for book design. We would also like to thank our Great Dames Board and Giving Circle members who invest in our work to empower women. Finally, thanks to Great Dames co-founders (and Sharon's daughters), Heather Cassey and Deirdre Hake, and to one of the most supportive partners in the world, Glenn Hake.

do?" "Run!" she said. I did and I made my flight.

I am sharing this story because it was such a learning moment for me. The moral goes beyond the idea that persistence pays off. Instead, it crystalized something I have known for a long time: My own power comes from offering somebody else the chance to be powerful. Every time, I asked *"If it were possible, what would I do?,"* I helped open up their minds to possibilities, and they gave me the advice that let me accomplish what all said was impossible.

We are inclined to say no, it can't be done. Unfortunately, saying no stops us from finding the possible. Asking if it is possible opens us up to great things. We asked if it was possible to sail around the world. We asked if it was possible to fly. We asked if it was possible to go to the moon. And we did all those things. Yet, on issues that threaten our planet and the people on it, we so often say "No" instead of asking "What if?" How can we think that women's equality is not possible? Why are we still working on world peace after hundreds of years? Why do we believe it's impossible to end hunger or poverty?

The truth is that all these things are solvable. All are possible. The problem is we do not have leaders who see possibilities. People are hungry, yet 70% of the food produced on the planet never gets to the table. It's not the lack of food that causes people to be hungry. It's a lack of leadership to distribute food. If you look at leadership, it's primarily management. It's not leading at all. It's managing what's there, rather than asking — what is possible for me to lead?

That's why I focus on creating future leaders. Many of the members of the World Academy come from villages in rural China where possibilities do not seem to exist. We ask them to go beyond their personal and geographic boundaries. This is what I tell them: "You're in your boundaries and what's beyond looks impossible. It looks like you're at your maximum, yet you're just at a point of possibility. Ask if it is possible and listen to how that could show up. It can come from somebody else